1 Discovering FRENCH Today!

Bleu

MW00933641

Lectures pour tous

with Test Preparation

HOLT McDOUGAL

HOUGHTON MIFFLIN HARCOURT

ISBN   978-0-547-87258-2
4 5 6 7 8 9 10   0928   21 20 19 18 17 16
4500605946   A B C D E F G

Table of Contents

Lectures supplémentaires

Academic and Informational Reading

Test Preparation Strategies

Introducing *Lectures pour tous*

Lectures pour tous
is a new kind of reading text.
As you will see, this book helps
you become an active reader.
It is a book to mark up, to
write in, and to make your
own. You can use it in class
and take it home.

Reading Skills Improvement— in French *and* English

You will read selections from your textbook, as well as great literature. In addition, you will learn how to understand the types of texts you read in classes, on tests, and in the real world. You will also study and practice specific strategies for taking standardized tests.

Help for Reading

Many readings in French are challenging the first time you encounter them. ***Lectures pour tous*** helps you understand these readings. Here's how.

Avant de lire The page before each reading gives you background information about the reading and a key to understanding the selection.

Reading Strategy Reading strategies help you decide how to approach the material.

What You Need to Know A preview of every selection tells you what to expect before you begin reading.

Reading Tips Useful, specific reading tips appear at points where language is difficult.

À réfléchir... Point-of-use, critical-thinking questions help you analyze content as you read.

À marquer This feature invites you to mark up the text by underlining and circling words and phrases right on the page.

Grammaire As you read, this feature highlights key grammar concepts.

Vocabulaire This feature helps you with the new vocabulary as you read the selection.

Analyse littéraire This feature appears in the *Lectures supplémentaires* section and encourages you to focus on one aspect of literary analysis as you read.

Reader's Success Strategy These notes give useful and fun tips and strategies for comprehending the selection.

Challenge These activities keep you challenged, even after you have grasped the basic concepts of the reading.

Vocabulary Support

Mots clés Important new words appear in bold. Their definitions appear in a *Mots clés* section at the bottom of any page where they occur in the selection. You will practice these words after the selection.

Vocabulaire de la lecture Vocabulary activities follow each selection and give you the opportunity to practice the *Mots clés.* Active vocabulary words appear in blue.

Comprehension and Connections

Tu as compris? Questions after each selection check your understanding of what you have just read.

Connexion personnelle These short writing activities ask you to relate the selection to your life and experiences to make what you have read more meaningful.

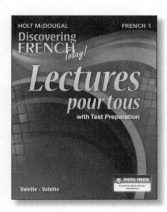

Links to *Discovering French, Today!*

When using ***Discovering French, Today!,*** you will find ***Lectures pour tous*** to be a perfect companion. ***Lectures pour tous*** lets you mark up the *Entracte* selections as you read, helping you understand and remember more.

Read on to learn more!

Academic and Informational Reading

Here is a special collection of real-world examples—in English—to help you read every kind of informational material, from textbooks to technical directions. Why are these sections in English? Because the strategies you learn will help you on tests, in other classes, and in the world outside of school. You will find strategies for the following:

Analyzing Text Features This section will help you read many different types of magazine articles and textbooks. You will learn how titles, subtitles, lists, graphics, many different kinds of visuals, and other special features work in magazines and textbooks. After studying this section you will be ready to read even the most complex material.

Understanding Visuals Tables, charts, graphs, maps, and diagrams all require special reading skills. As you learn the common elements of various visual texts, you will learn to read these materials with accuracy and skill.

Recognizing Text Structures Informational texts can be organized in many different ways. In this section you will study the following structures and learn about special key words that will help you identify the organizational patterns:
• Main Idea and Supporting Details
• Problem and Solution
• Sequence
• Cause and Effect
• Comparison and Contrast
• Persuasion

Reading in the Content Areas You will learn special strategies for reading social studies, science, and mathematics texts.

Reading Beyond the Classroom In this section you will encounter applications, schedules, technical directions, product information, Web pages, and other readings. Learning to analyze these texts will help you in your everyday life and on some standardized tests.

Test Preparation Strategies

In this section, you will find strategies and practice to help you succeed on many different kinds of standardized tests. After closely studying a variety of test formats through annotated examples, you will have an opportunity to practice each format on your own. Additional support will help you think through your answers. You will find strategies for the following:

Successful Test Taking This section provides many suggestions for preparing for and taking tests. The information ranges from analyzing test questions to tips for answering multiple-choice and open-ended test questions.

Reading Tests: Long Selections You will learn how to analyze the structure of a lengthy reading and prepare to answer the comprehension questions that follow it.

Reading Tests: Short Selections These selections may be a few paragraphs of text, a poem, a chart or graph, or some other item. You will practice the special range of comprehension skills required for these pieces.

Functional Reading Tests These real-world texts present special challenges. You will learn about the various test formats that use applications, product labels, technical directions, Web pages, and more.

Revising-and-Editing Tests These materials test your understanding of English grammar and usage. You may encounter capitalization and punctuation questions. Sometimes the focus is on usage questions such as verb tenses or pronoun agreement issues. You will become familiar with these formats through the guided practice in this section.

Writing Tests Writing prompts and sample student essays will help you understand how to analyze a prompt and what elements make a successful written response. Scoring rubrics and a prompt for practice will prepare you for the writing tests you will take.

Entracte

Point-of-use comprehension support helps you read selections from *Discovering French, Nouveau!* and develop critical-thinking skills.

Reading Strategy
This feature provides reading tips and strategies that help you effectively approach the material.

What You Need to Know
This section provides a key to help you unlock the selection so that you can understand and enjoy it.

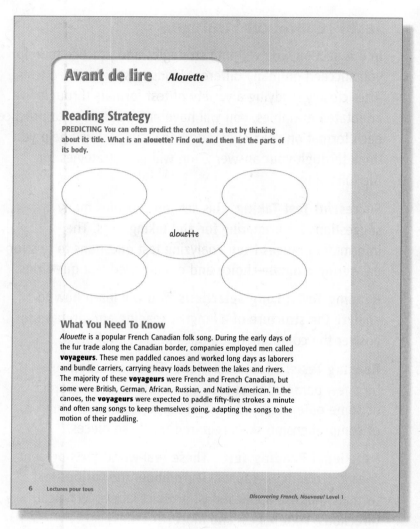

Avant de lire   *Alouette*

Reading Strategy
PREDICTING You can often predict the content of a text by thinking about its title. What is an **alouette**? Find out, and then list the parts of its body.

alouette

What You Need To Know
Alouette is a popular French Canadian folk song. During the early days of the fur trade along the Canadian border, companies employed men called **voyageurs**. These men paddled canoes and worked long days as laborers and bundle carriers, carrying heavy loads between the lakes and rivers. The majority of these **voyageurs** were French and French Canadian, but some were British, German, African, Russian, and Native American. In the canoes, the **voyageurs** were expected to paddle fifty-five strokes a minute and often sang songs to keep themselves going, adapting the songs to the motion of their paddling.

6   Lectures pour tous

Discovering French, Nouveau! Level 1

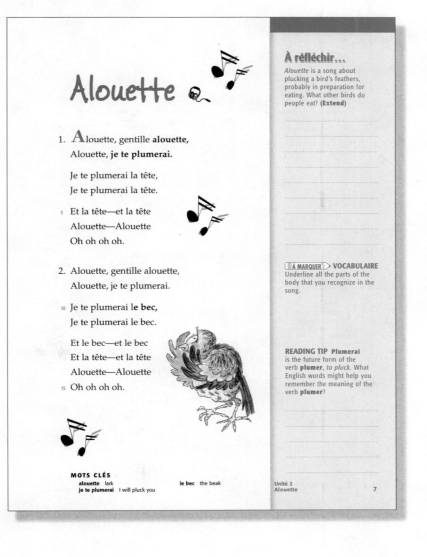

Alouette

À réfléchir...

Alouette is a song about plucking a bird's feathers, probably in preparation for eating. What other birds do people eat? **(Extend)**

1. **A**louette, gentille **alouette,**
   Alouette, **je te plumerai.**

   Je te plumerai la tête,
   Je te plumerai la tête.

5 Et la tête—et la tête
   Alouette—Alouette
   Oh oh oh oh.

2. Alouette, gentille alouette,
   Alouette, je te plumerai.

10 Je te plumerai **le bec,**
   Je te plumerai le bec.

   Et le bec—et le bec
   Et la tête—et la tête
   Alouette—Alouette
15 Oh oh oh oh.

A MARQUER VOCABULAIRE
Underline all the parts of the body that you recognize in the song.

READING TIP Plumerai
is the future form of the verb **plumer**, *to pluck.* What English words might help you remember the meaning of the verb **plumer**?

MOTS CLÉS
alouette lark
je te plumerai I will pluck you

le bec the beak

Unité 2
Alouette

7

À réfléchir...
Point-of-use questions check your understanding and ask you to think critically about the passage.

A MARQUER
VOCABULAIRE
This feature helps you with the new vocabulary as you read the selection. Underlining or circling the example makes it easy for you to find and remember.

MOTS CLÉS
Important vocabulary words appear in bold within the reading. Definitions are given at the bottom of the page.

READER'S SUCCESS STRATEGY

Notes like this one provide ideas to help you read the selection successfully. For example, some notes suggest that you fill in a chart while you read. Others suggest that you mark key words or ideas in the text.

CHALLENGE

This feature asks you to expand upon what you have learned for enrichment.

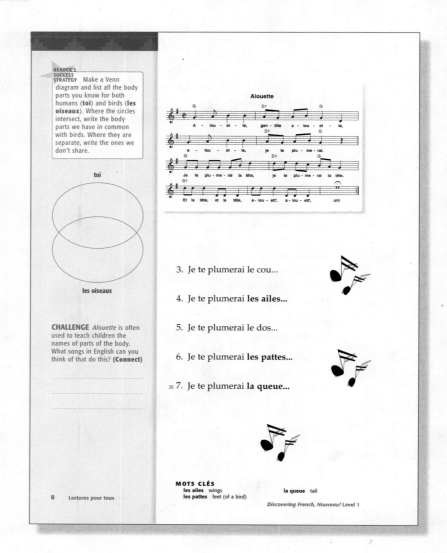

READER'S SUCCESS STRATEGY Make a Venn diagram and list all the body parts you know for both humans (**toi**) and birds (**les oiseaux**). Where the circles intersect, write the body parts we have in common with birds. Where they are separate, write the ones we don't share.

toi

les oiseaux

CHALLENGE *Alouette* is often used to teach children the names of parts of the body. What songs in English can you think of that do this? **(Connect)**

Alouette

A - lou - et - te, gen - tille a - lou - et - te,
a - lou - et - te, je te plu - me - rai.
Je te plu - me - rai la tête, je te plu - me - rai la tête.
Et la tête, et la tête, a - lou - ett', a - lou - ett', oh!

3. Je te plumerai le cou...

4. Je te plumerai **les ailes...**

5. Je te plumerai le dos...

6. Je te plumerai **les pattes...**

20 7. Je te plumerai **la queue...**

MOTS CLÉS
les ailes wings
les pattes feet (of a bird)
la queue tail

Discovering French, Nouveau! Level 1

8   Lectures pour tous

Vocabulaire de la lecture

Mots clés

une alouette *lark*	**les pattes** *feet (of a bird)*
plumer *to pluck*	**la tête** *head*
le bec *beak*	**le cou** *neck*
la queue *tail*	**le dos** *back*
les ailes *wings*	**gentil(le)** *nice, sweet*

A. Label the parts of the **alouette's** body.

B. Match the verb on the left with the appropriate noun on the right.

_____ **1.** manger *(to eat)*   a. les ailes

_____ **2.** voler *(to fly)*   b. le bec

_____ **3.** marcher *(to walk)*   c. la tête

_____ **4.** penser *(to think)*   d. la queue

_____ **5.** se secouer *(to shake)*   e. les pattes

Unité 2
Alouette

9

Vocabulaire de la lecture
Vocabulary practice follows each reading, reinforcing the *Mots clés* that appear throughout the selection. Words that appear in blue are *leçon* vocabulary words in ***Discovering French, Nouveau!***

Tu as compris?
Comprehension questions check your understanding and provide the opportunity to practice new vocabulary words.

Connexion personnelle
These short writing activities help you see connections between what happens in the selection and in your own life.

Tu as compris?

1. Comment s'appelle l'oiseau?

_____

2. Comment est l'alouette?

_____

3. Quelles parties du corps *(body)* sont mentionnées?

_____

Connexion personnelle

French Canadian fur trappers sang songs to keep themselves going. Do you know a song that keeps you going? Write two sentences like this:

J'écoute (listen to) la chanson (song) / musique _____ .

_____

_____

_____

_____

Lectures supplémentaires

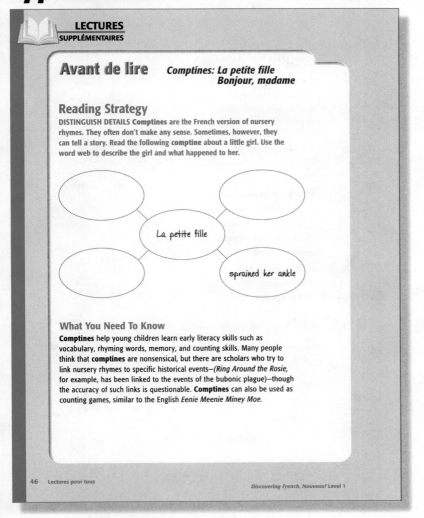

LECTURES SUPPLÉMENTAIRES

Avant de lire
Comptines: La petite fille
Bonjour, madame

Reading Strategy
DISTINGUISH DETAILS Comptines are the French version of nursery rhymes. They often don't make any sense. Sometimes, however, they can tell a story. Read the following **comptine** about a little girl. Use the word web to describe the girl and what happened to her.

La petite fille

sprained her ankle

What You Need To Know
Comptines help young children learn early literacy skills such as vocabulary, rhyming words, memory, and counting skills. Many people think that **comptines** are nonsensical, but there are scholars who try to link nursery rhymes to specific historical events—*(Ring Around the Rosie,* for example, has been linked to the events of the bubonic plague)—though the accuracy of such links is questionable. **Comptines** can also be used as counting games, similar to the English *Eenie Meenie Miney Moe.*

46   Lectures pour tous

Discovering French, Nouveau! Level 1

Reading Strategy
This feature provides reading tips and strategies that help you effectively approach the material.

What You Need to Know
This section provides a key to help you unlock the selection so that you can understand and enjoy it.

À MARQUER > GRAMMAIRE

This feature asks you to notice how a particular grammar concept from the *leçon* is illustrated. Underlining or circling the example makes it easy for you to find and remember.

La petite fille

Une petite fille
sur[1] **une balançoire**
qui[2] **se tord la cheville**
et perd[3] la mémoire.

5 Un monsieur lui dit[4]:
«Comment t'appelles-tu?»
Elle répond: «Tant pis[5],
je ne m'en souviens plus[6],
est-ce que c'est Juliette
10 est-ce que c'est Juliane
est-ce que c'est Mariette
est-ce que c'est Mariane?
Mais ce que je sais[7],
je le sais bien:
15 Rue des Serins
numéro vingt
habite[8] un chien qui est **coquin**».

---

[1] on [2] who [3] loses [4] says
[5] too bad [6] I don't remember any more [7] what I know
[8] lives

MOTS CLÉS

une balançoire	swing	**la cheville**	ankle
se tord	sprains	**coquin**	mischievous, a rascal

LECTURES SUPPLÉMENTAIRES

À réfléchir...

Cross out the statement that is *not* true about *La petite fille*. **(Clarify)**

The little girl is on a swing.

A man asks the little girl what her name is.

The girl's name is Juliette.

The little girl tells the man that a mischievous dog lives at 20, rue des Serins.

À MARQUER > GRAMMAIRE
In *La petite fille*, underline the passage in which the man asks the girl what her name is. Then, write a sentence saying what your name is.

_____

_____

_____

READING TIP In French, direct and indirect object pronouns come before the verbs. In *La petite fille*, find the sentence, "Un monsieur lui dit" and "je le sais bien." Note the indirect and direct object pronouns **lui** and **le**.

READER'S SUCCESS STRATEGY **Comptines** are meant to be said out loud. Read *La petite fille* out loud and notice where the rhyme scheme changes. Circle this line.

Academic and Informational Reading

This section helps you read informational material and prepare for other classes and standardized tests.

Academic and Informational Reading

In this section you'll find strategies to help you read all kinds of informational materials. The examples here range from magazines you read for fun to textbooks to bus schedules. Applying these simple and effective techniques will help you be a successful reader of the many texts you encounter every day.

89

VARIED TYPES OF READINGS

The wide variety of academic and informational selections helps you access different types of readings and develop specific techniques for those reading types.

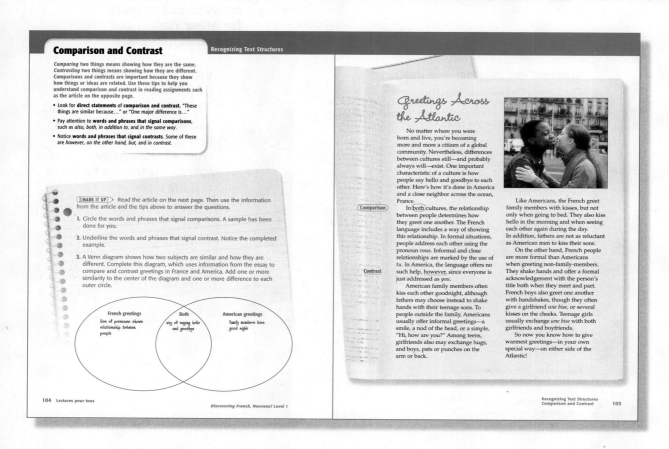

SKILL DEVELOPMENT

These activities offer graphic organizers, Mark It Up features, and other reading support to help you comprehend and think critically about the selection.

Test Preparation for All Learners

Lectures pour tous offers models, strategies, and practice to help you prepare for standardized tests.

NOTES

Reading Test Model
SHORT SELECTIONS

DIRECTIONS "Canada's Many Cultures" is a short informative article. The strategies you have just learned can also help you with this shorter selection. As you read the selection, respond to the notes in the side column.

When you've finished reading, answer the multiple-choice questions. Use the side-column notes to help you understand what each question is asking and why each answer is correct.

Canada's Many Cultures

Canada's people come from different cultures, and many wish to safeguard their special language and customs. Some French-speaking Canadians are separatists, or people who want the province of Quebec to become an independent country. In 1980 and 1995, separatists asked for a vote on whether Quebec should become independent. Both times the issue was defeated, but the separatists promised to try again.

Quebec's Importance The federal government wants Quebec to remain part of Canada. Quebec is responsible for half of Canada's aerospace production, half of its information technology, and 38 percent of its high-tech industry. French culture is important in Canada's history and modern-day identity.

Laws Protecting Multiculturalism The Quebec provincial government has passed laws to preserve its citizens' French heritage. In an attempt to satisfy the separatists,

READING STRATEGIES FOR ASSESSMENT

Find the main idea and supporting details. Circle the main idea of the article. Then underline the details that support the main idea.

Use context clues. To discover what a "separatist" is, study the words and phrases around it. Which phrase helps define it?

Notice important details. Underline details that explain the importance of industry in Quebec.

Discovering French, Nouveau! Level 1

TEST PREPARATION STRATEGIES

- Successful test taking
- Reading test model and practice—long selections
- Reading test model and practice—short selections
- Functional reading test model and practice
- Revising-and-editing test model and practice
- Writing test model and practice
- Scoring rubrics

Revising-and-Editing Test Model

DIRECTIONS Read the following paragraph carefully. Then answer the multiple-choice questions that follow. After answering the questions, read the material in the side columns to check your answer strategies.

¹Paris, the capital of France. ²It is home to one of that nations cultural treasures—the Louvre museum. ³The building was constructed in the thirteenth century as a fortress. ⁴Then they opened it there in 1783 today it has over 500,000 square feet of exhibition space. ⁵The museum is located on a street called the Rue de Rivoli. ⁶Their are many famous works of art they're, including the Venus de Milo and the Mona Lisa.

READING STRATEGIES FOR ASSESSMENT

Watch for common errors. Highlight or underline errors such as incorrect spelling or punctuation, fragments or run-on sentences, and missing or misplaced information.

ANSWER STRATEGIES

❶ Which sentence in the paragraph is actually a fragment, an incomplete thought?

   A. sentence 1
   B. sentence 3
   C. sentence 4
   D. sentence 5

Incomplete Sentences A sentence is a group of words that has a subject and a verb and expresses a complete thought. If either the subject or the verb is missing, the group of words is an incomplete sentence.

❷ In sentence 2, which of the following is the correct possessive form of the word *nation*?

   A. nation's
   B. nations's
   C. nations'
   D. nations

Possessive Nouns In sentence 2, the word *nation* is singular. So, it takes the singular possessive form.

Writing Test Model

DIRECTIONS Many tests ask you to write an essay in response to a writing prompt. A writing prompt is a brief statement that describes a writing situation. Some writing prompts ask you to explain *what, why,* or *how.* Others ask you to convince someone of something.

As you analyze the following writing prompts, read and respond to the notes in the side columns. Then look at the response to each prompt. The notes in the side columns will help you understand why each response is considered strong.

Prompt A

   Some child-rearing experts believe that young people should be kept busy after school and on the weekends with a variety of structured activities, such as music lessons, sports, dance classes, and so on. Others say that young people today have been "overscheduled" and need more time to themselves—to read, think about the future, and even just to daydream.

   Think about your experiences and the way your non-school time is structured. Do you think lots of structure, more personal time, or a combination of the two is most beneficial to young people? Remember to provide solid reasons and examples for the position you take.

Strong Response

   Today was a typical day for my little brother Jeff. He got up at five o'clock to go to the local ice rink for hockey practice. Then he was off to school. At the end of the school day,

NOTES

ANALYZING THE PROMPT

Identify the focus. What issue will you be writing about? Circle the focus of your essay in the first sentence of the prompt.

Understand what's expected of you. First, circle what the prompt asks you to do. Then identify your audience. What kinds of details will appeal to this audience?

ANSWER STRATEGIES

Capture the reader's interest. The writer begins by describing a typical busy day in his younger brother's life.

Avant de lire   *Frère Jacques*

Reading Strategy

ACTIVATE PRIOR KNOWLEDGE Many words can have a double meaning. **Soeur** can mean both "sister," as in a relative, and "Sister," as in a religious nun. What word in the song can have a double meaning? Write the word and its meaning in the box.

What You Need To Know

In the 10th and 11th centuries, when monasteries played a crucial role in medieval culture, canonical time—or the times of day dedicated to prayer—influenced the development of our current understanding of time. **Matins** referred to the morning prayer time (although these prayers were originally observed when it was still technically night—around 2:00 A.M.). Water clocks were used to power the bells, **les matines**, that rang out prayer time, and the monks who had water duty were afraid of sleeping through their job. Around the year 1300, mechanical clocks were developed in order to provide greater accuracy, and these clocks provided the blueprint for the clocks we use today.

Frère Jacques

Frère Jacques,
Frère Jacques,
Dormez-vous?
Dormez-vous?
5 **Sonnez les matines.**
Sonnez les matines.
Din! Din! Don!
Din! Din! Don!

À réfléchir...

Why do you think Frère Jacques couldn't wake up? **(Infer)**

⬛️ À MARQUER ⮞ **GRAMMAIRE**
You've learned that one of the ways to say "you" in French is **tu**. Underline another word in the song that means "you."

READING TIP Les matines comes from the word **matin**, meaning "morning." In English, we have the word **matinée**, which usually refers to a show or performance that takes place during the day, before the normally scheduled performance. Can you think of English words that might help you remember the meaning of the word **dormir?**

READER'S SUCCESS STRATEGY In French, one way to write questions is to invert subject and verb. Underline a question in the song.

CHALLENGE Describe how bells such as the ones described in this song might have been used in medieval monasteries. **(Draw conclusions)**

MOTS CLÉS
dormez sleep / are sleeping
sonnez ring
les matines the morning bells

Vocabulaire de la lecture

Mots clés

dormez   *sleep / are sleeping*

sonnez   *ring*

les matines   *the morning bells*

un frère   *brother*

vous   *you*

A. Complete the song with the missing words.

_____ Jacques,

_____ Jacques,

_____ -vous?

Dormez-_____

Sonnez _____

_____ les matines.

Din! Din! Don!

Din! Din! Don!

B. Fill in each blank with the appropriate vocabulary word.

1. _____ Jacques dort *(is sleeping)*.

2. C'est le matin! _____ les matines!

3. Comment allez- _____

Tu as compris?

1. Comment s'appelle le Frère?

_____

2. Est-il français ou américain?

_____

3. Qui est Jacques?

_____

Connexion personnelle

Imagine you are just meeting your tour guide, Jean-Luc, at the famous former monastery Mont Saint-Michel. Write a dialogue in which you greet him, introduce yourself, and find out his name. Ask him how he is doing.

_____

_____

_____

_____

_____

Avant de lire   *Alouette*

Reading Strategy
PREDICTING You can often predict the content of a text by thinking about its title. What is an **alouette**? Find out, and then list the parts of its body.

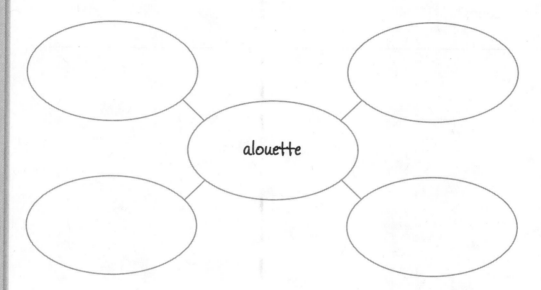

alouette

What You Need To Know
Alouette is a popular French Canadian folk song. During the early days of the fur trade along the Canadian border, companies employed men called **voyageurs**. These men paddled canoes and worked long days as laborers and bundle carriers, carrying heavy loads between the lakes and rivers. The majority of these **voyageurs** were French and French Canadian, but some were British, German, African, Russian, and Native American. In the canoes, the **voyageurs** were expected to paddle fifty-five strokes a minute and often sang songs to keep themselves going, adapting the songs to the motion of their paddling.

Alouette

1. **A**louette, gentille **alouette,**
   Alouette, **je te plumerai.**

   Je te plumerai la tête,
   Je te plumerai la tête.

   5 Et la tête—et la tête
   Alouette—Alouette
   Oh oh oh oh.

2. Alouette, gentille alouette,
   Alouette, je te plumerai.

   10 Je te plumerai le **bec,**
   Je te plumerai le bec.

   Et le bec—et le bec
   Et la tête—et la tête
   Alouette—Alouette
   15 Oh oh oh oh.

MOTS CLÉS

alouette lark	**le bec** the beak
je te plumerai I will pluck you	

À réfléchir…

Alouette is a song about plucking a bird's feathers, probably in preparation for eating. What other birds do people eat? **(Extend)**

_____

_____

_____

_____

_____

_____

_____

║║║À MARQUER║║⟩ VOCABULAIRE

Underline all the parts of the body that you recognize in the song.

READING TIP **Plumerai** is the future form of the verb **plumer**, *to pluck.* What English words might help you remember the meaning of the verb **plumer**?

_____

_____

_____

_____

Make a Venn diagram and list all the body parts you know for both humans (**toi**) and birds (**les oiseaux**). Where the circles intersect, write the body parts we have in common with birds. Where they are separate, write the ones we don't share.

toi

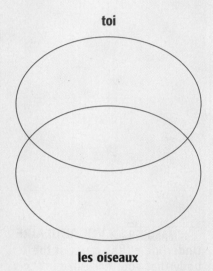

les oiseaux

CHALLENGE *Alouette* is often used to teach children the names of parts of the body. What songs in English can you think of that do this? (**Connect**)

Alouette

A - lou - et - te, gen - tille a - lou - et - te,
a - lou - et - te, je te plu - me - rai.
Je te plu - me - rai la tête, je te plu - me - rai la tête.
Et la tête, et la tête, a - lou - ett', a - lou - ett', oh!

3. Je te plumerai le cou...

4. Je te plumerai **les ailes**...

5. Je te plumerai le dos...

6. Je te plumerai **les pattes**...

20 7. Je te plumerai **la queue**...

MOTS CLÉS
les ailes wings
les pattes feet (of a bird)
la queue tail

Vocabulaire de la lecture

Mots clés

une alouette *lark*

plumer *to pluck*

le bec *beak*

la queue *tail*

les ailes *wings*

les pattes *feet (of a bird)*

la tête *head*

le cou *neck*

le dos *back*

gentil(le) *nice, sweet*

A. Label the parts of the **alouette's** body.

B. Match the verb on the left with the appropriate noun on the right.

_____ **1.** manger *(to eat)*   a. les ailes

_____ **2.** voler *(to fly)*   b. le bec

_____ **3.** marcher *(to walk)*   c. la tête

_____ **4.** penser *(to think)*   d. la queue

_____ **5.** se secouer *(to shake)*   e. les pattes

Tu as compris?

1. Comment s'appelle l'oiseau?

_____

2. Comment est l'alouette?

_____

3. Quelles parties du corps *(body)* sont mentionnées?

_____

Connexion personnelle

French Canadian fur trappers sang songs to keep themselves going. Do you know a song that keeps you going? Write two sentences like this:

J'écoute (listen to) la chanson (song) / musique _____.

_____

_____

_____

Avant de lire   *Bonjour, Trinh!*

Reading Strategy

LOOK FOR COGNATES French words that look like English words and have similar meanings are called *cognates,* for example, **les maths** or **la permission.** Scan the reading for cognates and make a list here of the French words and their English equivalents.

FRENCH WORD	ENGLISH WORD

What You Need To Know

Collège is the equivalent of junior high or middle school, and includes the following levels: **sixième, cinquième, quatrième,** and **troisième**—the equivalents of sixth, seventh, eighth, and ninth grades, respectively. The curriculum for French **collèges** is standardized. Languages are given a high priority: Students take their first foreign language beginning in **sixième,** with four hours of class a week. Many students choose English as their first foreign language. In **quatrième,** students must choose their second foreign language, with three hours of class per week. Each student thus spends seven hours a week, for four years, studying a foreign language.

À réfléchir...

What do you and Trinh have in common? Make a list of your likes and dislikes. Where do you and Trinh share similar tastes, and where do you differ? (**Compare and Contrast**)

_____

_____

_____

_____

A MARQUER **GRAMMAIRE**
In this unit, you have learned how to use the verb **aimer** followed by an infinitive to say what people like and don't like to do. In the boxed text, underline all the sentences with **aimer** and an infinitive. Then, write three similar sentences below using **aimer** and an infinitive to say three things you like (or don't like) to do.

_____

_____

_____

_____

READING TIP Remember that the verb **faire** is an irregular verb, meaning "to do or make." But **faire** is also used in many expressions like **faire un match, faire un voyage, faire attention.** Circle two expressions with **faire** that Trinh uses when discussing sports.

Bonjour, Trinh!

Bonjour!

Je m'appelle Trinh Nguyen. J'ai 14 ans. J'habite à Paris avec ma famille. Je suis élève de troisième au **collège.** J'étudie beaucoup,

5 mais je n'étudie pas tout le temps[1]. Voici ce que j'aime faire.

J'aime les boums parce que j'adore danser. J'aime la musique. J'aime **surtout** le rock, le rap et le reggae. J'aimerais[2] jouer de la

10 guitare, mais **je ne sais pas.**

J'aime les sports. En hiver je fais du snowboard et en été je nage et je joue au tennis. (Je ne suis pas un champion, mais je joue assez bien.) J'aime jouer au basket, mais

15 je préfère jouer au foot. Le week-end, quand il fait beau, j'aime faire du roller[3] avec mes copains.

J'aime mon collège. J'aime l'anglais parce

20 que le prof est sympa[4].

[1] all the time
[2] would like
[3] to go in-line skating
[4] nice

MOTS CLÉS
un collège   middle school or junior high
surtout   especially
je ne sais pas   I don't know / don't know how

J'aime aussi l'histoire, mais je n'aime pas trop[5] les maths.

À la maison, j'aime écouter mes CD de rock. J'aime aussi regarder la télé. J'aime le
25 sport et les films d'aventures.

J'aime jouer aux jeux vidéo. Et, j'aime jouer aux jeux **d'ordinateur** sur l'ordinateur de ma mère mais avant, **je dois** demander la permission. J'aime surfer sur l'Internet et
30 **télécharger** de la musique. J'aime **envoyer** des mails à mes copains. Je n'aime pas chatter **en ligne** parce que je n'aime pas parler à des gens[6] que je ne connais[7] pas.

J'aime téléphoner à ma copine, mais je
35 ne téléphone pas souvent. (Mon père n'aime pas ça[8].) Et vous, qu'est-ce que vous aimez faire? Répondez-moi vite[9].

Amicalement[10],

Trinh

---

[5] too much	[6] people
[7] know	[8] that
[9] quickly	[10] In friendship

LES SPORTS	LA MUSIQUE

LA TÉLÉ	L'ORDINATEUR

CHALLENGE Do you think Trinh is someone you might like to get to know? Why or why not? **(Evaluate)**

_____

_____

_____

_____

_____

_____

MOTS CLÉS

un ordinateur computer
je dois I must
télécharger to download

envoyer to send
en ligne on line

Vocabulaire de la lecture

Mots clés

un collège *middle school or junior high*

surtout *especially*

je ne sais pas *I don't know / don't know how*

un ordinateur *computer*

je dois *I must*

télécharger *to download*

envoyer *to send*

en ligne *on line*

habiter *to live*

étudier *to study*

faire *to do*

assez bien *well enough*

A. Fill in each blank with the appropriate vocabulary word.

Je suis élève au _____. J'aime la musique, _____

le rock, le rap, et le reggae. J'aimerais jouer du piano, mais _____.

Je joue au tennis. Je ne suis pas champion, mais je joue _____.

J'aime surfer sur l'Internet sur l'_____ de mon père, mais

_____ demander la permission. J'aime chatter _____.

B. Match the verb on the left with the appropriate noun on the right.

_____ **1.** télécharger   a. un match

_____ **2.** envoyer   b. la ville

_____ **3.** habiter   c. de la musique

_____ **4.** étudier   d. un mail

_____ **5.** faire   e. l'espagnol

Tu as compris?

1. Pourquoi est-ce que Trinh aime les boums?

_____

2. Quelle sorte de musique est-ce qu'il aime?

_____

3. Qu'est-ce que Trinh aime faire en hiver? En été?

_____

4. Pourquoi est-ce qu'il aime l'anglais?

_____

5. À qui est-ce qu'il aime téléphoner?

_____

Connexion personnelle

Imagine that you are writing a response to Trinh's email. Using his email as a model, write and tell Trinh all about yourself. Be sure to write in French, and include your likes and dislikes.

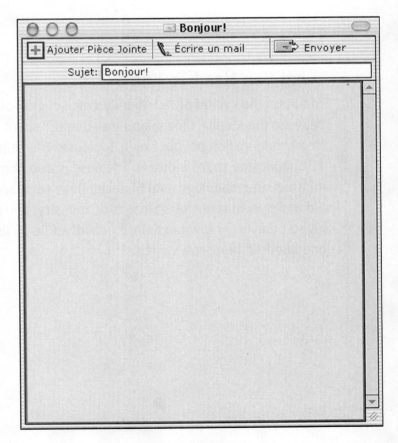

Avant de lire *Bonjour, Brigitte!*

Reading Strategy

SCAN Reading very quickly to get a specific piece of information is called scanning. Scan the reading and complete the family tree. Include one detail about each family member.

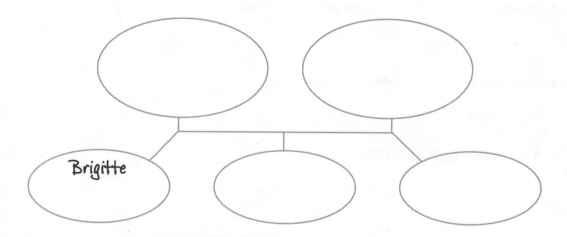

Brigitte

What You Need To Know

Toulouse, the capital of the Midi-Pyrénées region of France, is located between the Mediterranean and the Atlantic, about 400 miles from Paris. Nearly one million people live in Toulouse. The center of the French aeronautic and space industry, Toulouse is also home to electronics, information technology, and biotechnology companies. An interesting mix of old and new in terms of architecture, industry, and lifestyle, Toulouse is the biggest university town in France outside of Paris. Its universities serve over one hundred thousand students.

Bonjour, Brigitte!

Chers[1] copains américains,
Je m'appelle Brigitte
Lavie. J'ai quatorze ans.
Voici ma photo. Je ne suis
5 pas très grande, mais je
ne suis pas petite. Je suis
de taille[2] moyenne[3]. Je
suis brune, mais j'ai
les yeux verts. Je suis
10 sportive. J'aime le ski,
le jogging et la danse
moderne.

J'habite à Toulouse
avec ma famille. Mon
15 père travaille dans
l'industrie **aéronautique.**
Il est **ingénieur.** Ma
mère travaille dans une
banque. Elle est directrice[4]
20 du personnel.

[1] Dear   [2] size
[3] average   [4] director

À réfléchir...

1. Based on what you know from Brigitte's letter, which of the following items does she have? (**Clarify**)

☐ dog

☐ MP3 player

☐ television

☐ scooter

☐ computer

☐ moped

2. Describe what you think Brigitte is like. (**Infer**)

_____
_____
_____
_____
_____

⫼ À MARQUER⟩ VOCABULAIRE
In the boxed text, Brigitte describes her brother and sister and her dog, Attila. Circle the adjectives Brigitte uses to describe them.

READING TIP Notice all the different family members that Brigitte discusses. Underline all the ones that you see.

MOTS CLÉS
les yeux eyes
aéronautique aeronautical

ingénieur engineer

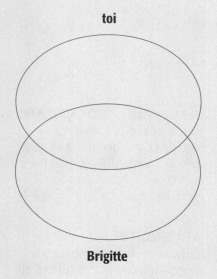

J'ai une soeur et un frère. Ma petite soeur s'appelle Élodie. Elle a cinq ans. Elle est très mignonne. Mon frère s'appelle Mathieu. Il a treize ans. Il est pénible. J'ai un

25 chien. Il s'appelle Attila mais il est très gentil. (Il est plus gentil que[5] mon frère!) J'ai aussi deux poissons rouges[6]. Ils n'ont pas de nom[7].

J'ai un lecteur MP3 et j'adore écouter de la musique. J'ai un ordinateur.

30 C'est **un cadeau** de ma marraine[8]. Je surfe sur l'Internet et **j'envoie** des mails. Je n'ai pas de scooter mais j'ai une mob.

J'ai beaucoup de copains, mais je n'ai pas de «**petit copain**». Ça n'a pas

35 d'importance[9]! Je suis **heureuse** comme ça[10].

Amitiés,

Brigitte

---

[5] nicer than   [6] goldfish   [7] name
[8] godmother   [9] It doesn't matter!   [10] like that

MOTS CLÉS
cadeau gift   **petit copain** boyfriend
j'envoie I send   **heureuse** happy

Vocabulaire de la lecture

Mots clés

les yeux *eyes*
aéronautique *aeronautical*
un ingénieur *engineer*
j'envoie *I send*
un cadeau *gift*

un petit copain *boyfriend*
heureuse *happy*
pénible *a pain*
mignonne *cute*
brune *dark-haired*
gentil *nice*

sportive *athletic*
grande *tall*
un lecteur MP3 *MP3 player*

A. Fill in each blank with the appropriate vocabulary word.

Chers amis,

Je suis à Paris chez mon oncle et ma tante. J'aime beaucoup mes cousines, ma

tante et mon oncle. Mon oncle travaille comme _____ dans l'industrie

_____. Mes cousines aiment les animaux, mais leur appartment est

petit. Elles ont un poisson rouge. C'est un _____ de ma tante. Ma

cousine Alice joue au tennis, fait du jogging, et en hiver, elle fait du ski. Elle est

_____. Elle a un _____ qui s'appelle Pierre. Elle aime la

musique, et elle a un _____. Elle a un ordinateur et _____

des mails à mes copains. Ma plus petite cousine a quatre ans. Elle a les _____

bleus. Elle est très _____.

À bientôt!

Sophie

B. Match each word with its opposite.

_____ **1.** triste   a. gentil

_____ **2.** petite   b. pénible

_____ **3.** méchant   c. heureuse

_____ **4.** blonde   d. grande

_____ **5.** sympathique   e. brune

Tu as compris?

1. Quel âge a Brigitte?

_____

2. Quels sports est-ce qu'elle aime?

_____

3. Où est-ce qu'elle habite?

_____

4. Que fait le père de Brigitte? Sa mère?

_____

5. Comment est sa soeur? Son frère?

_____

Connexion personnelle

Describe your best friend in the notebook.

Avant de lire *Bonjour, Ousmane!*
MC Solaar

Reading Strategy

GATHER AND SORT INFORMATION One way to gain understanding of a text is to gather and sort information as you read. What kinds of music do you and your classmates like and listen to? Interview two people and fill out this chart. Then, use the chart to gather information about Ousmane.

| Questions | Personne | | Ousmane |
	1	2	
Aimes-tu la musique?			
Quelle genre de musique préfères-tu?			
Qui est ton chanteur/ta chanteuse préféré(e)?			
Joues-tu d'un instrument de musique? Lequel?			

What You Need To Know

Senegal, located on the west coast of Africa, was once part of French West Africa. It gained its independence in 1960. Bordered by Mauritania in the north, by Mali in the east, and by Guinea and Guinea-Bissau in the south, Senegal is just a bit smaller than South Dakota. While French is its official language, Wolof, Pulaar, Diola, and Mandinka are among several other languages spoken by the Senegalese. The capital of Senegal is Dakar, also the country's largest city, located at the westernmost point of Africa. Senegal is known for its music; its rhythms have inspired all kinds of music around the world, from jazz to blues to reggae.

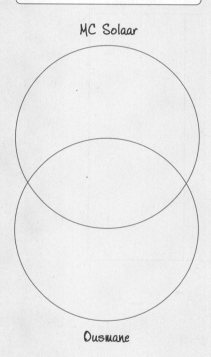

À MARQUER **VOCABULAIRE**
Reread the boxed text. Circle the different types of music mentioned.

READER'S SUCCESS STRATEGY Compare and contrast the two descriptions of Ousmane and MC Solaar. Use the Venn diagram to organize your ideas. Where the circles are separate, write in differences. Where they intersect, write in similarities.

MC Solaar

Ousmane

Bonjour, Ousmane!

Bonjour! Je m'appelle Ousmane. J'adore la musique. J'aime surtout le rap et le rock. Mon chanteur[1] préféré est MC Solaar. Il chante très bien. J'ai beaucoup de CD de lui. Ma soeur, elle, préfère le blues et le jazz.

5

Je suis un peu musicien. Je joue de la guitare. Et je ne joue pas trop mal. J'ai organisé[2] un petit orchestre[3] de rock avec des copains. Nous **répétons** le mercredi après-midi. Nous ne répétons pas chez moi, parce que ma mère déteste ça[4]. Parfois[5], le week-end, nous jouons à des boums pour nos amis.

10

15

[1] singer
[2] organized
[3] band
[4] that
[5] sometimes

MOTS CLÉS
répéter to rehearse

MC Solaar

le «Monsieur Rap» français

MC Solaar est né[6] à Dakar au Sénégal. Il s'appelle en réalité Claude M'Barali. Ses parents **émigrent** en France quand il a six mois. Il **fait ses études** dans la région parisienne. Après[7] **le bac,** il s'intéresse à[8] la musique. Il compose des chansons[9] françaises sur des rythmes de rap américain. Ses chansons ont beaucoup de succès. MC Solaar donne[10] des concerts en France, mais aussi en Angleterre[11], en Allemagne[12], en Russie et dans les pays[13] d'Afrique.

Aujourd'hui, MC Solaar est le «Monsieur Rap» français! Dans ses chansons, il exprime[14]

des messages positifs contre[15] la violence et pour la paix[16]. Voilà pourquoi il est très populaire en France et dans le monde[17] francophone.

[6] was born	[7] after
[8] becomes interested in	[9] songs
[10] gives	[11] England
[12] Germany	[13] countries
[14] expresses	[15] against
[16] peace	[17] world

MOTS CLÉS
émigrer to emigrate
faire ses études to go to school; studies
le bac short for **baccalauréat,** the exam at the end of **lycée** which guarantees university admittance
francophone French-speaking

À réfléchir...

1. Which of the following is not true of MC Solaar? Cross it out. **(Clarify)**

He was born in Dakar, Senegal.

He sings in French.

He sings rap music.

His songs are often about violence.

He is very popular in France and in the French-speaking world.

2. Ousmane is a very popular Senegalese name. Why might France be a popular location to which Senegalese people would choose to emigrate? **(Infer)**

_____

_____

_____

_____

READING TIP Remember to look for cognates, words that look alike in English and in French. What cognates do you find in *MC Solaar, le «Monsieur Rap» français?* Underline them in the text.

CHALLENGE MC Solaar is originally from Senegal. He sings rap in French. What other musicians do you know who blend musical traditions?

_____

_____

_____

Vocabulaire de la lecture

Mots clés

répéter *to rehearse*

émigrer *to emigrate*

faire ses études *to go to school; studies*

le bac *short for **baccalauréat,** the exam at the end of **lycée** which guarantees university admittance*

francophone *French-speaking*

jouer de *to play (a musical instrument)*

un concert *a concert*

la soeur *sister*

la guitare *guitar*

A. Match the verb on the left with the noun on the right with which it is best associated.

_____ **1.** émigrer

_____ **2.** jouer

_____ **3.** faire ses études

a. l'école

b. un pays

c. le piano

B. Fill in each blank with the appropriate vocabulary word.

1. Sénégal est un pays _____.

2. La fille de mon père et de ma mère est ma _____.

3. J'adore la musique! Ce week-end, je vais à un _____ pour écouter de la musique.

4. Après le lycée, beaucoup de jeunes Français passent *(take)* un examen qui

s'appelle le _____.

5. Ousmane joue de la _____.

6. Pour bien jouer du piano, il faut _____.

Tu as compris?

1. Quelle est la musique préférée d'Ousmane?

_____

2. Quand est-ce qu'il répète avec ses copains?

_____

3. Pourquoi est-ce qu'il ne répète pas à la maison?

_____

4. Où est né MC Solaar?

_____

5. Qu'est-ce qu'il exprime dans ses chansons?

_____

Connexion personnelle

Who is your favorite musician? Why?

Mon chanteur / Ma chanteuse

préféré(e) est...

_____

parce que...

_____

_____

_____

_____

_____

Avant de lire   *Les jeunes Français et la mode*

Reading Strategy

SKIM Before reading a long passage, it is helpful to read quickly to get a general idea of its content. Skim the paragraphs, noting clues that indicate the central theme or topic. By skimming, you can tell quickly what the reading is about. Then it will be easier to do a more careful reading. After skimming *Les jeunes Français et la mode,* write down some words or phrases that indicate what it is about.

_____

_____

_____

_____

_____

What You Need To Know

Paris has long been a fashion center of the world. Rue du Faubourg Saint-Honoré is one of the most famous streets for connoisseurs of **haute couture.** It is lined with the boutiques of French designers, including Lanvin, Hermes, St. Laurent, Givenchy, and Cardin. For shoppers with a bit less money to spend, the **Grands Magasins**[1]—for example, Galeries Lafayette and Printemps, located on the boulevard Haussman—are a must-see. For savvy shoppers who are pinching pennies, **les soldes**[2] take place twice a year, once in winter and once in summer. During these times—one-month periods determined by the French government—all clothing stores put their merchandise on sale, and there are tremendous deals to be had.

---

[1] department stores   [2] sales

Les jeunes Français et
LA MODE

Est-ce que vous aimez être à la mode[1]? Où est-ce que vous achetez vos vêtements? Et qu'est-ce qui compte[2] le plus[3] pour vous? le style? la qualité? le prix? Nous avons posé[4]
5 ces questions à cinq jeunes Français. Voilà leurs réponses.

---
[1] in style   [2] counts
[3] the most   [4] asked

Florence (16 ans)

J'aime être à la mode. Malheureusement[5], mon budget est limité. La solution? Le samedi après-midi je travaille dans **une boutique de**
10 **mode.** Là, **je peux** acheter mes jupes et mes pulls à des prix très avantageux[6]. Pour le reste, je compte sur la générosité de mes parents.

---
[5] unfortunately   [6] reasonable

MOTS CLÉS
une boutique de mode fashion boutique
je peux I can

À réfléchir...

1. Consider what you have learned about French young people and fashion. Do you and your friends share the same ideas with the French teenagers? Name some of the ideas you have in common and some ideas that are different. **(Compare and Contrast)**

READER'S SUCCESS STRATEGY To keep track of what each of the French teenagers says about buying clothes, use a chart like the one below. Highlight the strategies each of the teens uses to purchase clothes or be in fashion, then write them in the chart.

French Teenager	How he/she buys clothes
Florence	
Chloé	
Julien	
Robert	
Éric	

READING TIP Spoken language is different from written language. Spoken language can include slang expressions—for example, **C'est marrant; C'est génial.** Sometimes, in spoken French, the **ne** is dropped from a negative expression, as in **C'est pas cher** and **C'est pas drôle.**

Chloé (15 ans)

Pour moi, le style, c'est tout[7]. Hélas, la mode n'est pas bon marché. Heureusement[8], j'ai une
15 cousine qui a une machine à coudre[9] et qui est très adroite[10]. Alors, nous cousons[11] des rubans[12] et des patchs sur nos vêtements. De cette façon[13], nous **créons** notre propre[14] style. C'est génial, non?

[7] everything	[8] fortunately	[9] sewing machine
[10] skillful	[11] sew	[12] ribbons
[13] manner, way	[14] own	

Julien (14 ans)

20 Vous connaissez[15] le proverbe: «L'habit ne fait pas le moine*.» Eh bien, pour moi, les vêtements n'ont pas d'importance. Avec mon argent, je préfère acheter des CD. Quand j'ai besoin de jeans ou de tee-shirts, je vais aux
25 puces[16]. C'est pas cher et c'est marrant[17]!

[15] know	[16] flea market	[17] fun

* *Clothes don't make the man.*

MOTS CLÉS
créer to create

Robert (15 ans)

Aujourd'hui la présentation extérieure est très importante. Mais il n'est pas nécessaire d'être à la mode pour être bien habillé[18]. Pour moi, la qualité des vêtements est aussi importante 30 que leur style. En général, j'attends **les soldes.** J'achète peu de vêtements mais je fais attention à la qualité.

---
[18] dressed

Éric (12 ans)

Moi, je n'ai pas le choix[19]! C'est ma mère qui choisit mes vêtements. En ce qui concerne[20] la 35 mode, elle n'est pas dans le coup[21]. Elle achète tout sur catalogue et elle choisit ce qui est le moins cher[22]. C'est pas **drôle.**

---
[19] choice   [20] as for   [21] with it
[22] the cheapest (the least expensive)

MOTS CLÉS
un solde sale

drôle funny

À MARQUER ⟩ GRAMMAIRE
You've just learned how to make comparisons. In Robert's section, underline an example of a comparison.

CHALLENGE Which student shares the attitude towards fashion that is closest to yours? Explain why. (**Connect**)

Vocabulaire de la lecture

Mots clés

une boutique de mode *fashion boutique*

je peux *I can*

créer *to create*

un solde *sale*

drôle *funny*

le prix *the price*

un pull *sweater*

bon marché *cheap / inexpensive*

génial *terrific*

cher *expensive*

acheter *to buy*

A. Fill in each blank with the appropriate vocabulary word.

1. Florence travaille dans une _____.

2. Le style de Chloé et sa cousine est _____.

3. Robert attend les _____ pour acheter ses vêtements.

4. Quand la mère d'Éric achète ses vêtements, il trouve que cela

   n'est pas _____.

5. Selon ces jeunes Français, la mode n'est pas _____.

6. Puisque *(Since)* je suis riche, _____ acheter beaucoup
   de vêtements.

B. For each vocabulary word in the first column, find the sentence or phrase in the second column that best describes it. Write the corresponding letter in the blank.

_____ **1.** une boutique de mode

_____ **2.** un pull

_____ **3.** cher

_____ **4.** le prix

_____ **5.** acheter

_____ **6.** créer

a. Je le mets quand il fait froid.

b. On paie avec l'argent.

c. un endroit où on peut acheter
   des vêtements

d. pas bon marché

e. ce qu'on paie pour quelque chose

f. faire

Tu as compris?

1. Comment est-ce que Florence gagne son argent?

_____

2. Qu'est-ce que Chloé fait pour être à la mode?

_____

3. Est-ce que Julien aime être à la mode?

_____

4. Est-ce que Robert achète beaucoup de vêtements?

_____

5. Comment est-ce que la mère d'Éric achète les vêtements de son fils?

_____

Connexion personnelle

Imagine you are going on a trip to Paris. Make a list of the clothing items you might like to buy there. Include as much detail as you can.

Avant de lire   *Le roller: un sport qui roule!*

Reading Strategy

PREDICT Use titles and pictures to predict what a reading will be about. What can you tell about this reading from the title and the picture on page 34? What will you be learning about in this reading?

Look at	Learn
Title	
Pictures	

What You Need To Know

In-line skating was first invented by a Belgian in the early 18th century, as a way to replace ice-skating in the summer. The first pair of in-line skates were nothing more than a pair of boots with wooden cylinders attached to the bottom in a single line. The design of roller skates was perfected in the 19th century by a Frenchman and later, an American, but it wasn't until the 1980s, when two hockey players—brothers by the name of Olson—found an old pair of in-line skates and decided to replicate the design and sell their skates under the name of Rollerblade, Inc., that the sport gained in popularity.

Le roller: un sport qui roule![1]

Beaucoup de jeunes Français participent aux sports d'équipe[2] comme[3] le foot, le basket et le volley, mais certains préfèrent les sports individuels comme le jogging ou la natation.
5 Aujourd'hui, beaucoup de jeunes pratiquent aussi les «sports de glisse[4]» comme le roller, le skate, la planche à voile (en été) et le ski et le snowboard (en hiver).

Le roller est particulièrement populaire
10 parce qu'il peut être **pratiqué** en toute[5] saison et par **les gens** de tout âge. Deux millions de Français font régulièrement du roller, principalement dans les grandes villes et surtout[6] dans la région parisienne.
15 «Pour moi,» dit Clément, 15 ans, «le roller est l'occasion[7] de me faire des nouveaux copains.» Mélanie, 17 ans, dit qu'elle fait du roller «parce que j'ai l'impression de vitesse[8], d'indépendance et de liberté. Je suis libre[9]
20 comme un oiseau.» Pour Charlotte, 21 ans, «le roller est un excellent moyen[10] de faire de l'exercice et de rester en bonne forme[11] physique.»

---

[1] rolls   [2] team   [3] like   [4] gliding
[5] any   [6] above all   [7] opportunity   [8] speed
[9] free   [10] means   [11] shape

MOTS CLÉS
pratiqué practiced   **les gens** people

1. All of the following are mentioned as benefits of in-line skating except: **(Clarify)**

speed

saves money

doesn't pollute

competition

helps you stay in shape

2. Which of the following statements best summarizes the main idea of the reading? **(Main Idea)**

☐ In-line skating offers many advantages to someone who wants to stay in shape.

☐ In-line skating is a great way to get around cities.

☐ In-line skating is a fun but dangerous sport.

☐ In-line skating is a popular sport for many French young people which, when practiced safely, offers many benefits.

À MARQUER GRAMMAIRE
Many adverbs in French end in **–ment**, as many in English end in *–ly*. In the boxed section, underline three adverbs and write them here along with their English equivalents.

_____

_____

_____

L'équipement du roller!

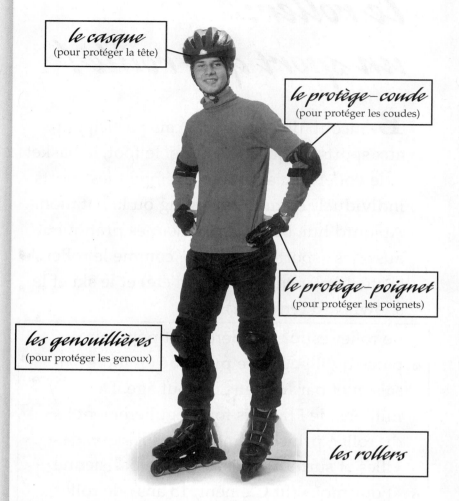

le casque
(pour protéger la tête)

le protège–coude
(pour protéger les coudes)

le protège–poignet
(pour protéger les poignets)

les genouillières
(pour protéger les genoux)

les rollers

Pour certaines personnes qui habitent dans
25 les grandes villes, le roller est un nouveau
moyen de transport urbain. Philippe Tardieu,
un jeune avocat[12] de la région parisienne, va
à son bureau[13] en roller. «Le roller est plus
économique, moins polluant[14] et souvent plus
30 rapide que l'auto. Le roller, ça roule...!»
Le roller a beaucoup d'avantages, mais c'est
aussi un sport qui peut être dangereux si on
ne fait pas attention. Pour faire du roller, on

---

[12] lawyer   [13] office   [14] polluting

doit être en bonne forme physique et avoir
35 l'équipement nécessaire. On doit toujours
porter un casque pour **se protéger** la tête. On
doit aussi porter des genouillières pour se
protéger les genoux[15] et des protège-poignets
pour se protéger les poignets[16].

40 On peut faire du roller dans la rue ou sur
toute surface **plane,** mais il est préférable de
pratiquer ce sport dans les endroits réservés
pour cette activité. Dans les grandes villes, il
y a des «rollerparks» où les jeunes peuvent
45 aussi faire du roller acrobatique et jouer au
hockey sur roller.

À Paris, une association sportive nommée
Pari-Roller organise tous les vendredis soirs[17]
une grande randonnée en roller dans les rues
50 de la ville. Cette randonnée[18] commence à dix
heures du soir et finit à une heure du matin. Il
y a souvent 12 000 (douze mille) participants
de tout âge accompagnés de policiers en roller.
Pendant cet **événement, les rues du circuit**
55 sont interdites[19] aux voitures. Pour beaucoup
de Parisiens, cet événement est l'occasion de
redécouvrir[20] leur ville dans une ambiance[21]
d'amitié, de bonne humeur et de **fête**
populaire.

[15] knees	[16] wrists	[17] every Friday evening
[18] long ride	[19] closed	[20] to rediscover
[21] atmosphere		

MOTS CLÉS
se protéger to protect (oneself)   **les rues du circuit** roadways
plane flat   **l'amitié** friendship
un événement event   **une fête** festival

READER'S SUCCESS STRATEGY Keep track of the reasons that different people have for in-line skating.

Clément

Mélanie

Charlotte

Philippe

CHALLENGE What kind of benefits might there be as a result of the Friday night in-line skating event in Paris? **(Infer)**

Vocabulaire de la lecture

Mots clés

pratiqué *practiced*

les gens *people*

se protéger *to protect (oneself)*

plane *flat*

un événement *event*

les rues du circuit *roadways*

l'amité *friendship*

une fête *festival*

faire du roller *do in-line skating*

le soir *evening*

le matin *the morning*

souvent *often*

A. Fill in each blank with the appropriate vocabulary word.

1. Le roller peut être dangereux. Il est important de _____.

2. Les randonnées du vendredi soir à Paris se passent dans une ambiance d'amitié et de _____ populaire.

3. Pendant les grandes randonnées à Paris, les _____ sont interdites aux voitures.

4. La randonnée à Paris est un grand _____ pour la ville.

5. On peut faire du roller sur toute surface _____.

6. Le roller peut être _____ en toute saison.

7. Les _____ de tous les âges pratiquent le roller.

B. For each vocabulary word in the first column, find the phrase in the second column that best describes it. Write the corresponding letter in the blank.

_____ 1. le matin

_____ 2. le soir

_____ 3. faire du roller

_____ 4. souvent

_____ 5. amitié

a. un sport actif pour tout le monde

b. le sentiment qu'on a pour ses copains

c. avant midi

d. après 6h

e. le contraire de rarement

Tu as compris?

1. Pourquoi le roller est-il particulièrement populaire parmi les «sports de glisse»?

_____

2. Où va Philippe Tardieu en roller?

_____

3. Nommez deux choses qui sont nécessaires avant de pratiquer le roller.

_____

4. Qu'est-ce qu'on peut faire dans des «rollerparks»?

_____

5. Combien de gens participent dans la grande randonnée à Paris tous les vendredis soirs?

_____

Connexion personnelle

What sport do you enjoy? Write down a sport that you like and list all its benefits.

Sport	Benefits

Avant de lire   *Bon appétit, Aurélie!*

Reading Strategy
SCAN Scan the list of pizzas on page 40 to see if there is one that a vegetarian might like to order. Write it here:

What You Need To Know
The French have always been known for their food and particularly for **haute cuisine,** a style of cooking developed by Auguste Escoffier. **Haute cuisine** is characterized by the refinement of French techniques and the organization of professional kitchens into a hierarchy of **chef** and **sous-chefs,** an arrangement still typical of most restaurant kitchens today. In the 1970s, a new style of French cooking emerged—**nouvelle cuisine**—which emphasized presentation and the use of herbs and spices instead of the traditional reliance on heavier sauces. Today, French cooking in general is much simpler and emphasizes fresh, local ingredients **(cuisine de terroir).** A typical French meal might start with a hot or cold **entrée** (starter, or hors d'oeuvre), followed by soup, main course, salad, cheese, and dessert. Wine or mineral water is usually served. There is a greater influence of foreign cooking, too, today, because of the many immigrants to France, particularly from North Africa and Asia.

Bon appétit, Aurélie!

Nous avons demandé à Aurélie de décrire ses repas.
Voici sa réponse.

À midi, je mange à **la cantine** de l'école
et le soir à la maison. C'est ma mère qui fait
les courses et c'est mon père qui prépare le
dîner. Il adore ça! Il fait une cuisine assez
5 traditionnelle, mais bien équilibrée[1]. En
général, on commence par une salade de
concombres ou de tomates. **Ensuite,** il y a
de la viande, par exemple, un bifteck ou du
poulet, avec des haricots verts ou des pommes
10 de terre. Parfois, on mange du
cassoulet[2] en boîte[3]. Après,
il y a une salade verte et des
fromages divers. Comme
dessert, il y a du yaourt ou un
15 fruit. Avec le repas, on boit de
l'eau minérale.

Quand
mon père
n'a pas envie
20 de faire la cuisine, on va
au restaurant. Dans notre

---

[1] balanced   [2] bean stew with pork or duck
[3] canned

MOTS CLÉS
la cantine cafeteria   ensuite next
un concombre cucumber

1. Based on what you know about Aurélie's eating habits, describe the ways in which your eating habits are similar to and different from Aurélie's. **(Compare and contrast)**

_____

_____

_____

_____

_____

⫴À MARQUER⟫ VOCABULAIRE
Reread the boxed section. Underline all the words that name a kind of meat, poultry, or vegetable.

READER'S SUCCESS STRATEGY   When reading instructions or other texts that involve steps, look for words like **ensuite** and **après** that indicate chronological order.

READING TIP Remember that in the United States, we use a different set of units for measuring both size and weight than many other countries, such as France, which use the metric system. If you look at the pizza menu, you'll notice that the size of the pizzas is given in **centimètres** (centimeters) instead of inches. Note, too, that the price is given in euros.

CHALLENGE Why do you suppose there might be more Vietnamese restaurants in France than Chinese restaurants? **(Draw conclusions)**

quartier, il y a un restaurant vietnamien que nous aimons bien. Mon **plat** préféré, c'est le riz avec des crevettes[4] et des petits pois.

25 Quand je sors avec mes copains, on va dans les fast-food. J'aime bien aller dans les pizzerias parce qu'on peut choisir ses ingrédients. En général, je prends une pizza avec du fromage, des olives et des **anchois.**

30 Avec la pizza, je bois souvent un soda.

[4] shrimp

ALLO *pizza*

MENU		26 cm 1 pers	31 cm 2/3 pers	40 cm 3/4 pers
italienne	sauce tomate, origan, mozzarella, anchois, olives	7,50€	12€	15€
4 saisons	sauce tomate, mozzarella, crème, olives, tomates fraîches, champignons	7,50€	12€	15€
3 fromages	sauce tomate, mozzarella, origan, chèvre, Roquefort	8€	13€	17€
pescatore	sauce tomate, mozzarella, origan, oignons, saumon, champignons	8€	13€	17€
anglaise	sauce tomate, mozzarella, origan, bacon, oeuf, pommes de terre	9€	14€	20€
texane	sauce tomate, mozzarella, origan, boeuf épicé, pepperoni, oignons	9€	14€	20€

02-47-66-89-89

PETIT DICTIONNAIRE

frais / fraîche fresh
boeuf épicé spicy beef
oignon onion
champignon mushroom
origan oregano
chèvre goat cheese
saumon salmon

MOTS CLÉS
un plat dish / meal

des anchois anchovies

Vocabulaire de la lecture

Mots clés

la cantine *cafeteria*
un concombre *cucumber*
ensuite *next*
un plat *dish / meal*
des anchois *anchovies*
faire les courses *to go shopping*

faire la cuisine *to do the cooking*
la viande *meat*
du poulet *chicken*
des pommes de terre *potatoes*
du yaourt *yogurt*
le riz *rice*

A. Fill in each blank with the appropriate vocabulary word.

1. Chez Aurélie, c'est sa mère qui _____ et son père

   qui _____.

2. À midi, Aurélie mange à la _____ de l'école.

3. Aurélie commence souvent son dîner avec une salade de concombres

   et _____, il y a de la _____.

4. Elle aime sa pizza avec du fromage, des olives, et des _____.

5. Au restaurant vietnamien, le _____ préféré d'Aurélie est le riz
   avec des crevettes et des petits pois.

B. Give an appropriate food item based on the description.

1. un oiseau qu'on peut manger _____

2. un légume qu'on mangeait tout le temps en Irlande _____

3. on le mange froid, avec une cuillière _____

4. un légume vert qu'on met souvent dans les salades _____

5. un petit grain blanc _____

Tu as compris?

1. Où est-ce qu'Aurélie mange à midi?

_____

2. Qui fait les courses chez Aurélie?

_____

3. Qui fait la cuisine chez Aurélie?

_____

4. Qu'est-ce qu'il y a comme dessert chez Aurélie?

_____

5. Quel type de restaurant est-ce qu'il y a dans le quartier d'Aurélie?

_____

Connexion personnelle

Using the list of ingredients seen in the menu on page 40, plus any other French words you know, design your own personal pizza. Give it an appropriate name.

Ma Pizza: _____

Ingrédients: _____

_____

_____

_____

_____

_____

_____

Lectures supplémentaires

Lectures supplémentaires

In this section you will find literary readings in French. Like the **Entracte** readings, the literary readings have reading strategies, reading tips, reader's success strategies, critical-thinking questions, vocabulary activities, comprehension questions, and a short writing activity to help you understand each selection.

Avant de lire

Comptines: La petite fille
Bonjour, madame

Reading Strategy

DISTINGUISH DETAILS Comptines are the French version of nursery rhymes. They often don't make any sense. Sometimes, however, they can tell a story. Read the following **comptine** about a little girl. Use the word web to describe the girl and what happened to her.

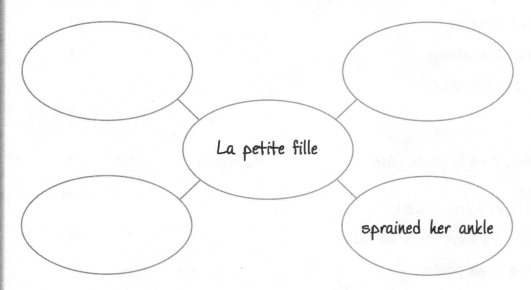

What You Need To Know

Comptines help young children learn early literacy skills such as vocabulary, rhyming words, memory, and counting skills. Many people think that **comptines** are nonsensical, but there are scholars who try to link nursery rhymes to specific historical events—(*Ring Around the Rosie,* for example, has been linked to the events of the bubonic plague)—though the accuracy of such links is questionable. **Comptines** can also be used as counting games, similar to the English *Eenie Meenie Miney Moe.*

La petite fille

Une petite fille
sur[1] **une balançoire**
qui[2] **se tord la cheville**
et perd[3] la mémoire.

5 Un monsieur lui dit[4]:
«Comment t'appelles-tu?»
Elle répond: «Tant pis[5],
je ne m'en souviens plus[6],
est-ce que c'est Juliette
10 est-ce que c'est Juliane
est-ce que c'est Mariette
est-ce que c'est Mariane?
Mais ce que je sais[7],
je le sais bien:
15 Rue des Serins
numéro vingt
habite[8] un chien qui est **coquin**».

---

[1] on [2] who [3] loses [4] says
[5] too bad [6] I don't remember any more [7] what I know
[8] lives

MOTS CLÉS
une balançoire swing
se tord sprains
la cheville ankle
coquin mischievous, a rascal

À réfléchir…

Cross out the statement that is *not* true about *La petite fille*. **(Clarify)**

The little girl is on a swing.

A man asks the little girl what her name is.

The girl's name is Juliette.

The little girl tells the man that a mischievous dog lives at 20, rue des Serins.

⫴ À MARQUER ⬎ GRAMMAIRE
In *La petite fille*, underline the passage in which the man asks the girl what her name is. Then, write a sentence saying what your name is.

_____

_____

_____

READING TIP In French, direct and indirect object pronouns come before the verbs. In *La petite fille*, find the sentence, "Un monsieur lui dit" and "je le sais bien." Note the indirect and direct object pronouns **lui** and **le.**

READER'S SUCCESS STRATEGY **Comptines** are meant to be said out loud. Read *La petite fille* out loud and notice where the rhyme scheme changes. Circle this line.

À MARQUER GRAMMAIRE

In *Bonjour, madame,* underline the passage in which someone asks the woman how she is feeling.

CHALLENGE What counting rhymes do you remember from your childhood that are similar to *La petite fille* and *Bonjour, madame?* How did you use them? **(Compare and Contrast)**

Bonjour, madame

— Bonjour, madame,

Comment ça va?

— Ça va pas mal.

Et votre **mari?**

5 — Il est **malade**

À la salade:

Il est guéri[9]

Au céleri.

———
[9] cured

MOTS CLÉS

un mari   husband   **malade**   sick

Vocabulaire de la lecture

Mots clés

une balançoire *swing*

se tord *sprains*

la cheville *ankle*

coquin *mischievous, a rascal*

un mari *husband*

malade *sick*

une fille *a girl*

un monsieur *a man*

madame *title for an older woman*
(similar to Mrs.)

un chien *a dog*

A. Fill in each blank with the appropriate vocabulary word.

1. La petite fille est sur une _____.

2. Elle _____ la cheville.

3. Le chien est _____.

4. Un _____ parle *(speaks)* avec la petite fille.

5. Le _____ est malade.

B. List the **mot clé** that is the closest in meaning to the *opposite* of the word given.

1. un garçon _____

2. bien _____

3. un chat _____

4. monsieur _____

5. le poignet *(wrist)* _____

Tu as compris?

1. Où est la fille?

Elle est _____

2. Est-ce qu'elle sait *(know)* son nom *(name)*?

_____

_____

3. Où habite le chien?

Il habite _____

4. Comment est le chien?

Il est _____

5. Comment est le mari?

Il est _____

Connexion personnelle

Imagine that you are on a trip to France. Write out a dialogue in which you meet another person. Introduce yourself and ask that person's name and how he or she is doing. Find out how old he or she is. Give the replies. Use dashes to indicate a change in speaker.

— Bonjour! Je m'appelle

Avant de lire

Savez-vous planter les choux?
Comptines: Bonjour
Les saisons

Reading Strategy

SCAN Scan the **comptines** for familiar words. Which words do you recognize? Write them here. What do they help you figure out about the **comptines**?

_____

_____

_____

_____

_____

_____

What You Need To Know

À la mode is a French term meaning *fashionable* or *chic.* Its original meaning, when found in the phrase, **à la mode de** ___, means *in the manner of* ___, and usually refers to a country or other place. In the United States, we use the term **à la mode** most often to mean *with ice cream* and it usually refers to apple pie served with vanilla ice cream. This American use was coined in the late 19th century by a diner in New York and made famous by a reporter in the *New York Sun.*

À réfléchir...

What other French expressions like **à la mode** do we use regularly in English? List a few here. How many others can you think of that have to do with food? **(Extend)**

_____

_____

_____

_____

_____

_____

_____

_____

READING TIP Nouns in French can sometimes be replaced by an object pronoun. In the song *Savez-vous planter les choux?*, notice the repeated line "on les plante". The object pronoun **les** refers to **les choux**.

READER'S SUCCESS STRATEGY Remember to read **comptines** out loud. *Savez-vous planter les choux?* is a song. Search the internet to get the music that goes along with the lyrics, and learn to sing the song.

Savez-vous planter les choux?

Savez-vous[1] **planter les choux?**
À la mode, à la mode,
Savez-vous planter les choux?
À la mode de chez nous[2]?

5 On les plante avec le doigt
À la mode, à la mode,
On les plante avec le doigt
À la mode de chez nous.

Savez-vous planter les choux?
10 À la mode, à la mode,
Savez-vous planter les choux?
À la mode de chez nous?

On les plante avec les mains…

On les plante avec le pied…

15 On les plante avec le coude…

On les plante avec le nez…

---
[1] Do you know
[2] our place / where we live

MOTS CLÉS
planter to plant   **les choux** cabbage

Bonjour

Bonjour, Madame Lundi,
comment va Madame Mardi?
— Très bien, Madame Mercredi;
dites[3] à Madame Jeudi
5 de **venir** vendredi
danser samedi
dans **la salle** de Dimanche.

[3] tell

Les saisons

Au printemps, p'tites[4] **feuilles**
En été, grandes[5] feuilles
En automne, plein d'[6]feuilles
En hiver, plus d'[7]feuilles.

[4] little	[5] big
[6] plenty of	[7] no more

MOTS CLÉS

venir to come
danser to dance

la salle room
les feuilles leaves

⫿⫿⫿À MARQUER⟩ VOCABULAIRE
In *Bonjour*, underline all
the days of the week. In *Les
Saisons*, underline the names
of all the seasons.

CHALLENGE In *Les Saisons*,
leaves are used as a symbol for
the changing of the seasons.
What else might you use to
represent the passage of time?
(Extend)

Vocabulaire de la lecture

Mots clés

planter *to plant*

les choux *cabbage*

venir *to come*

danser *to dance*

la salle *room*

les feuilles *leaves*

le printemps *the spring*

l'été *the summer*

l'automne *the fall*

l'hiver *the winter*

A. Match the word on the left with the appropriate phrase on the right.

_____ **1.** le printemps

_____ **2.** l'été

_____ **3.** l'automne

_____ **4.** l'hiver

a. il neige

b. mars, avril, mai

c. il fait très chaud

d. octobre, novembre

B. Fill in each blank with the appropriate vocabulary word.

1. Madame Lundi, Madame Mardi, Madame Mercredi, et Madame Jeudi

vont *(are going to)* _____ samedi.

2. Elles vont danser dans la _____ de Dimanche.

3. On plante les _____.

4. En été, il y a de grandes _____.

5. Madame Jeudi va *(is going to)* _____ vendredi.

6. On peut *(can)* _____ les choux avec le doigt.

Tu as compris?

1. Quelles parties du corps sont mentionées?

_____

2. Qui va danser?

_____

3. Où vont-elles danser?

_____

4. Qu'est-ce qu'on plante?

_____

5. En automne, est-ce qu'il y a plein de feuilles, ou plus de feuilles?

_____

Connexion personnelle

If you could write your own **comptine,** what might you write about? In the center of the web, write a subject for your **comptine.** Then brainstorm words you might associate with it.

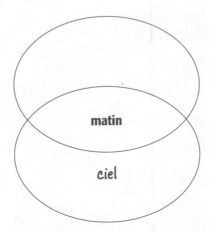

matin

ciel

Avant de lire

Sur le pont d'Avignon
La terre

Reading Strategy

PREDICT Look at the titles of the two short readings—the song *Sur le pont d'Avignon* and the poem *La terre.* Based on the titles, what do you think the readings will be about? Write your predictions in the following chart.

Sur le pont d'Avignon	
La terre	

What You Need To Know

The famous Avignon Bridge—or the bridge of St. Bénezet—was the first bridge to span the Rhône River, the dividing line between France and the Holy Roman Empire. Nearby, in Avignon, is the Popes' Palace.

Jacques Prévert, the author of *La terre,* was a French poet and screenwriter who lived from 1900–1977.

Sur le pont d'Avignon

Sur[1] **le pont** d'Avignon

L'on[2] y danse, l'on y danse,

Sur le pont d'Avignon

L'on y danse tout en rond[3].

5 Les beaux **messieurs** font comme ça[4]

Et puis encore[5] comme ça.

Sur le pont d'Avignon

L'on y danse tout en rond.

Sur le pont d'Avignon

10 L'on y danse, l'on y danse,

Sur le pont d'Avignon

L'on y danse tout en rond.

Les belles **dames** font comme ça

Et puis encore comme ça.

15 Sur le pont d'Avignon

L'on y danse tout en rond.

Les officiers font comme ça

Les bébés font comme ça

Les bons **amis** font comme ça

20 Les musiciens font comme ça

---

[1] on   [2] people   [3] in a circle
[4] like that   [5] then again

MOTS CLÉS
   le pont   the bridge   **les dames**   ladies
   les messieurs   gentlemen   **les amis**   friends

À réfléchir...

Sur le pont d'Avignon is a children's song. What English songs about bridges do you know? (**Compare and Contrast**)

_____

_____

_____

_____

READING TIP In many children's songs and poems, repetition is used to help foster understanding. Underline the repeated phrases in *Sur le pont d'Avignon.*

READER'S SUCCESS STRATEGY Don't worry if you can't understand every word in the song and poem. Read for the gist and for overall understanding. Use the words you do understand to help you with what you don't understand. Find a few words in the reading that you already know, or which you can understand because they look like English words, and write them here.

_____

_____

_____

_____

_____

À réfléchir...

In the poem *La terre*, why does the sun shine? **(Clarify)**

_____

_____

_____

_____

_____

▐▌▌▌ À MARQUER ⟫ **ANALYSE LITTÉRAIRE Personification** is a figure of speech that gives human characteristics to an inanimate object, or to an animal, or an idea. What is being personified in the poem *La terre*? Underline all the words that are being given human characteristics.

CHALLENGE How might you describe the behavior of the earth in the poem *La terre*? **(INFER)**

_____

_____

_____

_____

_____

_____

_____

À propos de l'auteur

Jacques Prévert est né *(born)* en 1900 à Neuilly-sur-Seine où il a grandi *(grew up)*. En 1920, il s'engage *(joined)* dans l'armée. Prévert a commencé à écrire *(to write)* dans les années 30. Il est l'auteur de poèmes, mais aussi de scénarios de films dont *(of which)* les plus connus *(known)* sont *Le Crime de M. Lange* (réalisateur Jean Renoir), et *Les enfants du paradis* (Marcel Carné). Il est mort *(died)* en 1977.

〜〜〜〜〜

La terre

La terre aime le soleil

et elle tourne

pour se faire admirer⁶

et **le soleil** la trouve⁷ belle

5   et il brille⁸ pour elle;

et quand il est fatigué

il va **se coucher**

et **la lune se lève.**

_____

⁶ to be admired
⁷ finds
⁸ shines

MOTS CLÉS

la terre the earth	**la lune** the moon
le soleil the sun	**se lève** gets up / rises
se coucher to go to bed / to set	

Vocabulaire de la lecture

Mots clés

le pont *the bridge*
les messieurs *gentlemen*
les dames *ladies*
les amis *friends*
la terre *the earth*

le soleil *the sun*
la lune *the moon*
se coucher *to go to bed / to set*
se lève *gets up / rises*
danse *dances*

et *and*
aime *loves*
pour *for*
est *is*

A. Fill in each blank with the appropriate vocabulary word.

1. Les gens dansent sur le _____.

2. Sur le pont d'Avignon, l'on y _____.

3. Les beaux _____ et les belles _____ font comme ça.

4. La terre _____ le soleil.

5. Quand le soleil est fatigué, il va se _____.

6. Quand le soleil se couche, la lune _____.

7. Le soleil brille _____ la terre.

8. Quand le soleil _____ fatigué, il va se coucher.

B. Say whether each statement is logical or illogical.

1. Voici Thomas et Sophie. Nous sommes amis.   L   I

2. La nuit, je regarde le soleil dans le ciel *(sky)*.   L   I

3. La terre brille pour la lune.   L   I

4. À une boum, on danse.   L   I

5. J'aime ma mère.   L   I

Tu as compris?

1. Où est le pont?

_____

2. Que font les gens sur le pont?

_____

3. Comment est-ce qu'ils dansent?

_____

4. Qui est-ce que la terre aime?

_____

5. Que fait le soleil quand il est fatigué?

_____

Connexion personnelle

How would you personify the wind if you were a poet? Brainstorm all the actions you associate with the wind.

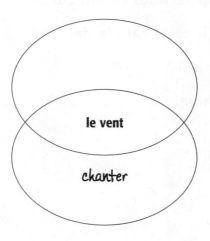

le vent

chanter

Avant de lire

Comptine: C'est la poule grise
La souris

Reading Strategy

SCAN Scan the **comptine** and the poem for the names of colors, and write them in this chart.

Les Couleurs

What You Need To Know

La souris was written by Lucie Delarue-Mardrus, a poet and novelist who lived from 1874 to 1945. She was born in Honfleur, in Normandy. Delarue-Mardrus was a prolific writer with more than seventy works to her name, including poems, novels, biographies, plays, short stories, and memoirs.

À réfléchir...

1. What do the **comptine** and the poem have in common? **(Compare and contrast)**

_____
_____
_____
_____
_____

READING TIP In many children's songs, as in poems, rhyme and rhythm are essential elements. Read the **comptine** and the poem out loud to get a good sense of both rhyme and rhythm.

READER'S SUCCESS STRATEGY Write in the words that rhyme with the following colors:

grise _____

noire _____

brune _____

blanche _____

C'est la poule grise

C'est **la poule** grise

Qui **pond** dans l'église[1];

C'est la poule noire

Qui pond dans l'armoire[2];

5 C'est la poule brune

Qui pond dans la lune;

C'est la poule blanche

Qui pond sur la planche[3].

---

[1] church [2] cupboard [3] board

MOTS CLÉS
la poule hen   **pond** lays (an egg)

À propos de l'auteur

Née en Normandie en 1874, Lucie Delarue-Mardrus était à la fois *(at the same time)* poétesse, romancière *(novelist)* et dessinatrice *(illustrator)*. Elle est surtout *(above all)* connue pour ses romans *(novels)* populaires comme *Ex-Voto,* consacré *(dedicated)* à la vie des gens de Honfleur, sa ville natale. Comme Colette, Delarue-Mardrus a célébré la naissance *(birth)* de la femme moderne du début du vingtième siècle.

La souris

C'est la petite **souris** grise,
dans **sa cachette** elle est assise[4],
quand elle n'est pas dans son **trou,**
c'est qu'elle galope partout[5].

5 C'est la petite souris blanche
qui **ronge le pain** sur la planche,
aussitôt qu'[6]elle entend[7] **du bruit,**
dans sa maison elle s'enfuit[8].

C'est la petite souris brune
10 qui **se promène** au clair de lune[9],
si le chat **miaule** en dormant[10],
elle **se sauve** prestement[11].

[4] seated [5] everywhere [6] as soon as
[7] hears [8] flees [9] moonlight
[10] while sleeping [11] nimbly

MOTS CLÉS

la souris mouse
sa cachette her hiding place
le trou hole
ronge gnaws
le pain bread

du bruit noise
se promène takes a walk
miaule meows
se sauve runs away / escapes

À MARQUER ▷ VOCABULAIRE
In each of the boxed sections of the poem *La souris,* underline an action that seems out of character for a mouse.

CHALLENGE There is a well-known saying, "When the cat's away, the mice will play." What actions in the poem *La souris* illustrate this saying? **(Analyze)**

Vocabulaire de la lecture

Mots clés

la poule   *hen*
pond   *lays (an egg)*
sa cachette   *hiding place*
la souris   *mouse*
le trou   *hole*
ronge   *gnaws*
le pain   *bread*

du bruit   *noise*
se promène   *takes a walk*
miaule   *meows*
se sauve   *runs away / escapes*
c'est...   *it's*
grise   *grey*
noire   *black*
blanche   *white*

A. Fill in each blank with the appropriate vocabulary word.

1. La poule _____ pond dans l'église.

2. La poule blanche _____ sur la planche.

3. La poule _____ pond dans l'armoire.

4. La souris blanche ronge _____ sur la planche.

5. La souris brune _____ au clair de lune.

6. La petite souris grise est assise dans sa _____ quand

   elle n'est pas dans son _____.

7. _____ la souris blanche qui s'enfuit quand

   elle entend _____.

B. Match the activity on the left with the appropriate animal on the right.

_____ **1.** miaule   a. la souris

_____ **2.** pond   b. le chat

_____ **3.** ronge   c. la poule

_____ **4.** se promène

_____ **5.** se sauve

Tu as compris?

1. Où pond la poule noire?

_____

2. Qui pond dans la lune?

_____

3. Que fait la souris grise quand elle n'est pas dans son trou?

_____

4. Où va la souris blanche quand elle entend du bruit?

_____

5. Comment est-ce que la souris brune se sauve si le chat miaule?

_____

Connexion personnelle

Write your own verse about a mouse of a certain color. Use the last stanza of the poem as a model. Don't worry if it doesn't make sense; play with rhyme and rhythm.

C'est la souris

Qui aime

Si le chat

Elle

Avant de lire   *Comptines: Un éléphant se balançait*
Trois poules

Reading Strategy

LOOK FOR CONTEXT CLUES At first, there might seem to be many words in the reading you can't understand. To improve your comprehension, use this strategy: read each sentence as a whole rather than translating word for word. Remember, too, to look for familiar words and see how they can help you figure out the meaning of unfamiliar ones. Fill in the box with words that you recognize.

What You Need To Know

Nursery rhymes and **comptines** are among the first songs children hear and thus, the rhymes and songs play an important role in language learning. A common characteristic of **comptines** is repetition. Many revolve around animals and nonsensical situations. Many **comptines,** such as these two, are used to help children learn to count.

Un éléphant se balançait

Un éléphant **se balançait**
Sur **une toile d'araignée;**
Il y trouva tant d'agrément[1]
Qu'il alla[2] chercher un deuxième éléphant.

5 Deux éléphants se balançaient
Sur une toile d'araignée
Ils y **trouvèrent** tant d'agrément
Qu'ils allèrent[3] **chercher** un troisième éléphant.

Trois éléphants…

10 Quatre éléphants…

Cinq éléphants…

Six éléphants…

Sept éléphants…

Huit éléphants…

15 Neuf éléphants…

Dix éléphants…

[1] He liked it so much there (literally: he found so much pleasantness there)
[2] he went
[3] they went

MOTS CLÉS
se balancer to swing
une toile d'araignée spider web
trouver to find
chercher to look for

À réfléchir…

1. How do these **comptines** help children learn to count? **(Draw conclusions)**

2. What nursery rhyme or song do you remember using to learn to count? **(Compare and contrast)**

A MARQUER **GRAMMAIRE**
You've learned how to conjugate the verb **aller** *(to go)*. In the boxed sections of the first **comptine**, look for words that look like they might be forms of the verb **aller** and underline them. Find forms of **aller** in the second **comptine** and underline them. Conjugate the verb **aller** here:

READING TIP The first **comptine** uses a verb form called the **passé simple,** which is sometimes called the literary past tense. The **passé simple** is no longer a spoken tense, but is often found in literature. Note the forms of **aller: alla,** and **allèrent.** Find the **passé simple** of the verb **trouver** and circle the two forms.

Trois poules

Quand trois poules s'en vont[3] aux **champs**

La première va devant.

La seconde suit[4] la première,

La troisième va derrière.

5 Quand trois poules s'en vont aux champs

La première va devant.

_____

[3] go   [4] follows

CHALLENGE Why do you think so many **comptines** involve animals? **(Infer)**

_____

_____

_____

_____

_____

_____

_____

MOTS CLÉS
les champs fields

Vocabulaire de la lecture

Mots clés

se balancer   *to swing*

une toile d'araignée   *spider web*

trouver   *to find*

chercher   *to look for*

les champs   *fields*

aller   *to go*

première   *first*

deuxième   *second*

troisième   *third*

A. Fill in each blank with the appropriate vocabulary word.

1. Les éléphants aiment _____ sur une _____.

2. Les poules s'en vont aux _____.

3. La _____ va devant.

4. La _____ va derrière.

5. Il alla chercher un _____ éléphant.

B. Write sentences using the verbs **aller, chercher, trouver.**

1. _____

2. _____

3. _____

Tu as compris?

1. Où est l'éléphant?

_____

2. Est-il content ou triste?

_____

3. Qu'est-ce qu'il fait?

_____

4. Où vont les poules?

_____

5. Qui va devant?

_____

Connexion personnelle

Imagine your own situation for a counting rhyme that involves an animal in a silly scenario. Write your ideas here.

L'animal	Que fait-il?

Avant de lire

Comptines: Sur le fil à sécher le linge
Mère-Mouton
Mes pantoufles

Reading Strategy

WORD CHOICE Writers choose words carefully in order to express their thoughts accurately. Through careful word choice, writers can help readers visualize an image or feel a certain way. As you read *Mes pantoufles*, think about how certain words and phrases affect you as a reader. Use the chart below to record interesting words and phrases and what they convey to you.

Words and Phrases	Ideas and Feeling They Convey

What You Need To Know

Mes pantoufles is a poem written by Anne-Marie Chapouton, a writer who was born in France and who spent parts of her childhood in Tunisia, Holland, and in the United States. She received her degree in French literature from Columbia University and returned to France in 1964, where she began a long career in children's literature.

À réfléchir...

1. What is the tone of the poem *Mes pantoufles* (page 73)? **(Analyze)**

_____

_____

2. Why does Mère Mouton threaten to knit her children's clothes from the father's wool? **(Clarify)**

_____

_____

_____

_____

> **READER'S SUCCESS STRATEGY** As you read the two **comptines** and the poem, highlight all the pieces of clothing that are mentioned. Sort them into the following categories.
>
> **Wear on your feet**
>
> _____
>
> _____
>
> **Wear on your body / arms**
>
> _____
>
> _____
>
> **Wear on your legs**
>
> _____
>
> _____

Sur le fil à sécher le linge

Sur **le fil à sécher le linge**
il y a un pantalon
c'est à mon cousin Gaston.

Sur le fil à sécher le linge
5 il y a un pull-over
c'est celui[1] de Philibert.

Sur le fil à sécher le linge
il y a quatre chaussettes
deux à moi, deux à Josette.

_____
[1] the one (m.)

Mère-Mouton

Madame mouton **tricote**
des manteaux pour ses enfants.
Six manteaux, six paire de bottes
pour ses six petits enfants.
5 — Cette année **la laine** est chère,
dit Mère-Mouton en bêlant[2],
six cache-nez[3], six pull-overs,

_____
[2] bleating   [3] nose-warmers

MOTS CLÉS
le fil à sécher le linge clothesline   **la laine** wool
tricoter to knit

ça coûte beaucoup d'argent.

Et s'il fait froid cet hiver

10 je tricoterai, mes enfants,

la laine de votre père

et celle[4] de l'oncle Fernand.

[4] the one (f.)

~~~~~~~~~~

À propos de l'auteur

Anne-Marie Chapouton (1939-2000) était originaire du sud de
la France. Elle a consacré sa vie à la littérature pour enfants.
Elle a écrit des romans et des poèmes (comme *Poèmes petits*),
mais également *(also)* des albums, en collaboration avec de
nombreux illustrateurs contemporains.

Mes pantoufles

Mes pantoufles

sont en **or,**

en **velours,**

en **soie** des Indes[5].

5 Mes pantoufles

sont des **fées**

qui m'attendent

sans **bouger.**

[5] from India (Indian)

MOTS CLÉS

une pantoufle a slipper	**la soie** silk
l'or gold	**une fée** a fairy
le velours velvet	**bouger** to move, to budge

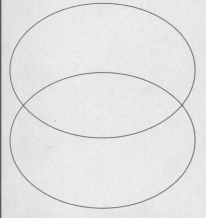

⫸À MARQUER⫷ ANALYSE LITTÉRAIRE A metaphor is a comparison between two things that doesn't use "like" or "as." Underline the metaphor in the poem *Mes pantoufles*. Name the two things being compared.

_____

_____

_____

_____

CHALLENGE How are the slippers described in the poem like slippers you wore as a child? Use the Venn diagram to record your answer. Where the circles are separate, write in differences. Where they intersect, write in similarities.

Mes pantoufles

Slippers from my childhood

Quand je rentre

10 de l'école

avec une

cabriole[6]

je les enfile[7]

à mes pieds.

15 Mes pantoufles

sont en or,

en velours,

en soie des Indes.

Mes pantoufles

20 sont des fées

qui **chauffent**

mes petits pieds.

_____

[6] somersault   [7] I slip them on

MOTS CLÉS
chauffer to warm

Vocabulaire de la lecture

Mots clés

le fil à sécher le linge   *clothesline*

tricoter   *to knit*

la laine   *wool*

une pantoufle   *a slipper*

l'or   *gold*

le velours   *velvet*

la soie   *silk*

une fée   *a fairy*

bouger   *to move, to budge*

chauffer   *to warm*

un manteau   *coat*

un pantalon   *pants*

un pull-over   *sweater*

des chaussettes   *socks*

A. Match the piece of clothing on the left with the appropriate description on the right.

_____ **1.** les pantoufles

_____ **2.** un manteau

_____ **3.** un pull-over

_____ **4.** un pantalon

    a. On le met pour aller dehors quand il fait froid.
       On le met sur les autres vêtements.

    b. En automne, je le porte quelquefois avec un jean.

    c. Je les mets sur mes pieds dans la maison.

    d. On peut le porter pour aller à l'école.
       Les garçons et les filles peuvent le porter.

B. Choose three vocabulary words and write a sentence with each one.

_____

_____

_____

_____

_____

Tu as compris?

1. À qui est le pull-over sur le fil à sécher le linge?

_____

2. Combien de chaussettes est-ce qu'il y a sur le fil à sécher le linge?

_____

3. Qu'est-ce que Madame Mouton tricote pour ses six enfants?

_____

4. Comment est la laine cette année?

_____

5. Comment sont les pantoufles?

_____

Connexion personnelle

What ordinary everyday item might you write a poem about? Decide on a subject for your poem and write a list of words and phrases you would use to describe it in the notebook at the right.

Avant de lire   *Auprès de ma blonde*

Reading Strategy

SKIM Look over the entire reading to get a sense of what it might be about. As you're skimming, look for familiar words. In this particular case, the text is a song, so look, too, for clues as to how it might be sung. Write your predictions here:

_____

_____

_____

_____

_____

_____

_____

What You Need To Know

Auprès de ma blonde is a French folk song that dates from the 17th century and is credited, in some instances, to André Joubert. Monsieur Joubert lived on the French island of Noirmoutiers, which was occupied by the Dutch in 1674 while France and England waged war against them. Joubert and six other men were captured and brought to Amsterdam where they were kept as hostages for two years before being released. An early version of this song appeared in 1704 under the title *Prisonnier de Hollande.* As is common for folk songs, *Auprès de ma blonde* has gone through many lyric changes. It is claimed as a traditional folk song by the Cajuns, the Québecois, and the Acadians. It was also taken up by French soldiers during World War II and sung as a peace song. **Une blonde** is slang for a *girl* or *girlfriend*.

À réfléchir...

1. How many speakers are there in the song? **(Clarify)**

_____

_____

2. Based on what you've read in the song, which of the following are true? Check three. **(Summarize)**

☐ The singer's father has a beautiful garden.

☐ The dove sings for girls who aren't married.

☐ The singer isn't married.

☐ The singer's husband is in Holland.

READER'S SUCCESS STRATEGY _Auprès de ma blonde_ is a folk song in the "call and response" tradition. Each successive verse starts with the last line of the previous verse and usually repeats it and introduces a new one. That way, a leader can sing the new line at the end of each verse and everyone else can join in afterwards to continue singing. To read this song like a poem, skip the repeated lines and read through to get a sense of one continuous story—or in this case—dialogue.

Auprès de ma blonde

Dans **les jardins** d'mon père

Les lilas sont fleuris[1].

Dans les jardins d'mon père

Les lilas sont fleuris.

5 Tous les oiseaux du monde

Vienn'nt y faire **leurs nids**[2].

Refrain

Auprès de[3] ma blonde qu'il fait bon, fait bon, fait bon

10 Auprès de ma blonde qu'il fait bon dormir!

Tous les oiseaux du monde

Vienn'nt y faire leurs nids

Tous les oiseaux du monde

Vienn'nt y faire leurs nids

15 **La caille, la tourterelle**

Et la jolie **perdrix**.

... Et ma jolie **colombe**

Qui chante jour et nuit.

---

[1] bloomed   [2] come make their nests there
[3] next to

MOTS CLÉS

les jardins gardens	**la tourterelle** turtledove
les lilas lilacs	**la perdrix** partridge
les nids nests	**la colombe** dove
la caille quail	

Qui chante pour les filles
20 Qui n'ont pas de mari.

… Pour moi ne chante guère[4]
Car j'en ai un joli[5].
… Dites-nous donc la belle
Où donc est votr'mari?

25 … Il est dans la Hollande,
Les Hollandais l'ont pris.

… Que donneriez-vous[6], belle
Pour avoir votr'mari?

… Je donnerais Versailles,
30 Paris et Saint-Denis.

… Les tours de Notre-Dame
Et l'clocher[7] d'mon pays.

… Et ma jolie colombe
Qui chante jour et nuit.

[4] hardly
[5] because I have a handsome one
[6] would you give
[7] church tower

Lectures supplémentaires
Auprès de ma blonde

À MARQUER > GRAMMAIRE
You've learned to use the passé composé with avoir. Read the boxed stanza and underline the sentence in the passé composé.

READING TIP When singing in French, you usually pronounce vowels that aren't pronounced when speaking French. For example, the word monde, when spoken, has a silent –e at the end but would be pronounced mon-de when sung. Vowels not to be sung are replaced with apostrophes.

CHALLENGE Why is the girl singing about her father's garden? (Draw conclusions)

Vocabulaire de la lecture

Mots clés

les jardins *gardens*

les lilas *lilacs*

les nids *nests*

la caille *quail*

la tourterelle *turtledove*

la perdrix *partridge*

la colombe *dove*

le jour *day*

la nuit *night*

A. Match the vocabulary word on the left with the appropriate description on the right.

_____ **1.** les lilas

_____ **2.** la colombe

_____ **3.** un jardin

_____ **4.** la caille

_____ **5.** un nid

a. C'est un oiseau qu'on peut manger.

b. C'est une maison pour oiseaux.

c. Ce sont des fleurs violettes qui sentent *(smell)* bonnes.

d. C'est un oiseau blanc, utilisé comme symbole pour la paix.

e. C'est un endroit avec beaucoup de fleurs.

B. Write one sentence for each of the remaining vocabulary words.

_____

_____

_____

_____

Tu as compris?

1. À qui est le jardin?

_____

2. Quel fleur est-ce qu'il y a dans le jardin?

_____

3. Que fait tous les oiseaux là-bas?

_____

4. Pourqui est-ce que la colombe chante?

_____

5. Où est le mari de la chanteuse? Pourquoi?

_____

Connexion personnelle

How might you describe your backyard or garden? What words or phrases would you choose to describe what happens there? Make a list here.

Mon jardin

Avant de lire
Comptines: **En allant chercher mon pain**
Monsieur de Saint-Laurent
Les bonbons

Reading Strategy

CONNECT TO YOUR OWN LIFE You can connect the subject of a reading to your own life. As you read these **comptines,** think about foods that you like to eat. Compare the foods mentioned as preferences in *Les bonbons* and write your own list of favorite foods.

Les Bonbons	My Preferences

What You Need To Know

The French are famous for the high value they place on food. **Gourmandise** is a French term that appears to have several meanings. According to Jean Anthelme Brillat-Savarin, who wrote *The Physiology of Taste* in 1826, **gourmandise** is the "passionate preference, well-determined and satisfied, for objects which flatter our taste" and not, as some dictionaries seemed to suggest, a "confusion of gluttony and voracity." Still, today **gourmandise** can mean either of the following:
1) a taste and relish for good food;
2) to overeat or eat immodestly, make a pig of oneself.

En allant chercher mon pain

En allant chercher mon pain

Je rencontre trois lapins,

Je les mets dans mon panier[1],

Ils me boivent tout mon lait;

5   Je les mets dans mon placard[2],

Ils me mangent tout mon **lard;**

Je les mets au coin du feu[3],

Ils me font trois petits oeufs,

   Bleu, blanc, rouge.

~~~~~~~~~~

Monsieur de Saint-Laurent

Monsieur de Saint-Laurent,

La canne en argent[4],

Le bouton doré[5],

Qu'avez-vous mangé?

5   — J'ai mangé un oeuf,

La moitié[6] d'un **boeuf,**

Quatre-vingts moutons,

Autant de[7] **chapons;**

J'ai bu la rivière,

10 Et j'ai encore faim!

— Monsieur de Saint-Laurent,

Vous êtes un gourmand.

---

[1] basket   [2] closet   [3] in a corner of the hearth
[4] silver cane   [5] golden button [6] half   [7] as many

MOTS CLÉS
le lard bacon
le boeuf beef

le chapon capon (a type
of chicken)

À réfléchir...

1. Number the phrases to show the order in which the rabbits in the first **comptine** do the following things. **(Chronological order)**

_____ lay three eggs

_____ drink milk

_____ eat the bacon

2. According to the second **comptine,** what is the definition of a **gourmand?** **(Draw conclusions)**

_____

_____

_____

_____

À MARQUER GRAMMAIRE
In this unit, you've learned to use direct object pronouns. In the first **comptine,** underline the phrases with direct object pronouns.

READING TIP These **comptines** contain a lot of familiar food vocabulary. Some new words you can figure out, such as **les vermicelles** (which is a cognate). Although it doesn't mean the exact same thing as the English word, **le lard** means _bacon_, which is definitely related.

Tu as compris?

1. Qu'est-ce que les lapins ont bu?

_____

2. Qu'est-ce que les lapins ont mangé?

_____

3. Combien de moutons est-ce que Monsieur de Saint-Laurent a mangé?

_____

4. Qu'est-ce qu'il a bu?

_____

Connexion personnelle

Make a list of foods that you like. List them on the chart and write a couple of reasons why you like each one.

La Nourriture	Les Raisons

Academic and
Informational Reading

Academic and Informational Reading

In this section you'll find strategies to help you read all kinds of informational materials. The examples here range from magazines you read for fun to textbooks to bus schedules. Applying these simple and effective techniques will help you be a successful reader of the many texts you encounter every day.

Reading a Magazine Article

A magazine article is designed to catch and hold your interest. You will get the most from your reading if you recognize the special features of a magazine page and learn how to use them. Look at the sample magazine article as you read each strategy below.

A Read the **title** to get an idea of what the article is about. Scan any other **headings** to see how information in the article is organized.

B As you read, notice any **quotations.** Who is quoted? Is the person a reliable source on the subject?

C Notice information set in special type, such as **italics** or **boldface.** For example, look at the quotation in the article that is set in italic type.

D Study **visuals,** such as charts, graphs, pictures, maps, and bulleted lists. Visuals add important information and bring the topic to life.

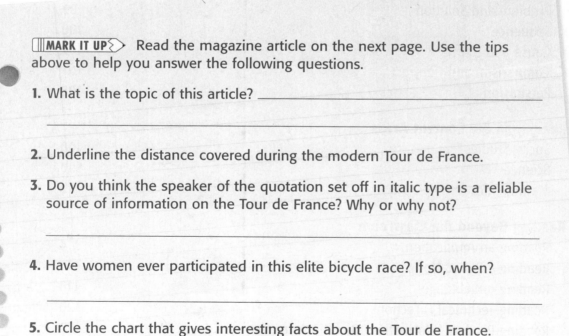

MARK IT UP Read the magazine article on the next page. Use the tips above to help you answer the following questions.

1. What is the topic of this article? _____
   _____

2. Underline the distance covered during the modern Tour de France.

3. Do you think the speaker of the quotation set off in italic type is a reliable source of information on the Tour de France? Why or why not?
   _____

4. Have women ever participated in this elite bicycle race? If so, when?
   _____

5. Circle the chart that gives interesting facts about the Tour de France.

A CYCLING'S SUPREME CHALLENGE— THE TOUR DE FRANCE

Everyone loves jumping on a bike and pedaling around for enjoyment and exercise. Increasing numbers of people even rely on cycling as their major means of transportation. But for those elite athletes whose lives revolve around cycling, there are just three words—Tour de France.

The idea for the Tour de France, the world's ultimate bicycle race, was hatched at a business lunch in Paris just over a century ago. It was based on a six-day track race, but with the riders wending their way through the country instead of going in circles. The first race, held in 1903, totaled 2,428 km.

Today, the race covers 3,427 km (2,100 miles) in 20 stages, or separate races, that begin and end in the same day. Each stage has a winner, and the rider with the lowest total time at the end of the three weeks becomes the overall champion. The cyclists race in

teams, with each team often working together to ensure that one of its members wins. The Tour is restricted to men, although races for women were held from 1984 to 1989.

C *"The Tour de France," says current Tour chief Jean-Marie Leblanc, "is an uncommon human adventure . . . ."*

Part of what makes the race such an unusual and exciting event is the fact that the fans don't have to go to it—it comes to them. People along the route can reach out and touch the cyclists, and have been known to hand racers a water bottle or even offer a helpful push.

France has given the world not only one of its most mouth-watering cuisines, but also the most athletically challenging way to work off all those calories. In the words of three-time Tour winner, American Greg LeMond, "You couldn't have this race in any other country." B

D

Number of chains worn out by a single rider		3
Youngest winner	20	Oldest winner	36
Average calories consumed by a rider per day		5,900
Total calories burned by a rider		123,900
Total number of pedal strokes		324,000 (at 60 rpm)
Winner's prize		€400,000

Add It Up—Tour Tidbits

Reading a Textbook

The first page of a textbook lesson introduces you to a particular topic. The page also provides important information that will guide you through the rest of the lesson. Look at the sample textbook page as you read each strategy below.

A Preview the **title** and other **headings** to find out the lesson's main topic and related subtopics.

B Read the **key ideas** or **objectives** at the top of the page. Keep these in mind as you read. They will help you set a purpose for your reading.

C Look for a list of terms or **vocabulary words** at the start of each lesson. These words will be identified and defined throughout the lesson.

D Study **visuals** such as photographs and illustrations. Read the **captions.** Visuals can add information and interest to the topic.

MARK IT UP Read the sample textbook page. Then use the strategies above to help you answer the following questions.

1. What is the topic of this lesson? _____

_____

2. Circle the key idea of the lesson.

3. Draw a box around the vocabulary words that will be defined in the lesson.

4. Put a star next to the visual that shows the structure of a sea arch.

5. Using a graphic organizer can help you take notes on the textbook material you learn. Complete the chart using information on shoreline features from the lesson.

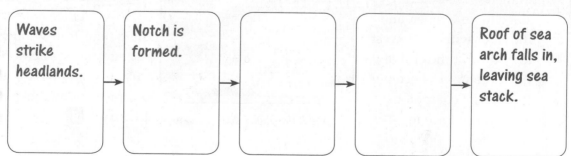

Waves strike headlands. → Notch is formed. → → → Roof of sea arch falls in, leaving sea stack.

A Shoreline Features

Ocean waves change the shape of a shoreline by eroding rock materials and by depositing sediments.

Waves and Erosion

Breaking storm waves may strike rock cliffs with a force of thousands of kilograms per square meter. Such breakers easily remove large masses of loose sand and clay. Air and water driven into cracks and fissures may split bedrock apart. Sand and pebbles carried by the water abrade the bedrock. Waves pound loose rock and boulders into pebbles and sand. In addition, seawater dissolves minerals from rocks such as limestone.

When waves strike the headlands of a deep-water shoreline, they may cut away the rock up to the high-tide level, forming a notch. If the materials overhanging the notch collapse, a sea cliff results.

Cliffs made of soft materials such as soil and sand wear away very quickly. For example, waves washing up on Cape Cod in Massachusetts are carrying away materials from sand cliffs there so rapidly that the cliffs are receding at a rate of about one meter every year.

In cliffs made of harder rock materials, a notch may deepen until it becomes a sea cave. Waves may cut through the walls of sea caves to form sea arches. Arches may also form when waves cut through vertical cracks in narrow headlands. If the roof of a sea arch falls in, what remains is a tall, narrow rock island called a sea stack.

Sea caves, sea arches, and sea stacks can be seen on the coasts of California, Oregon, Washington, and Maine, on the Gaspé Peninsula of Canada, and in many parts of the Mediterranean Sea.

16.3

B KEY IDEA

Waves erode shorelines and deposit sediments in characteristic formations.

C KEY VOCABULARY

- beach
- sandbar
- fjord

BAJA PENINSULA Ocean waves have formed this sea stack and sea arch in Mexico.

D

Sea arch

★

Reading a Table

Tables give a lot of information in an organized way. These tips can help you read a table quickly and accurately. Look at the example as you read each strategy in this list.

A Look at the **title** to find out the content of the table.

B Read the **introduction** to get a general overview of the information included in the table.

C Examine the **heading** of each row and column. To find specific information, locate the place where a row and column intersect.

B Water temperatures vary widely along the coasts of North America. This table shows the temperature of the water in March at seven beaches.

A **Average March Water Temperature at Eight Beaches (°F)**

Location	Temperature	Location	Temperature
Newport, RI	37	Seattle, WA	46
Ocean City, MD	42	Honolulu, HI	76
Freeport, TX	62	Juneau, AK	37
Oceanside, CA	58		

MARK IT UP Answer the following questions using the table of March water temperatures.

1. Which two beaches have the same water temperature? Circle the answers in the table.

2. What units are used to measure the water temperatures?

_____

_____

3. If you were planning a swimming vacation in March, what beach might you consider visiting?

_____

_____

Reading a Map

To read a map correctly, you have to identify and understand its elements. Look at the example below as you read each strategy in this list.

A Read the **title** to find out what the map shows.

B Study the **legend,** or **key,** to find out what symbols and colors are used on the map and what they stand for.

C Look at **geographic labels** to understand specific places on the map.

D Look at the **scale** to understand how distances on the map relate to actual distances.

E Locate the **compass rose,** or **pointer,** to determine direction.

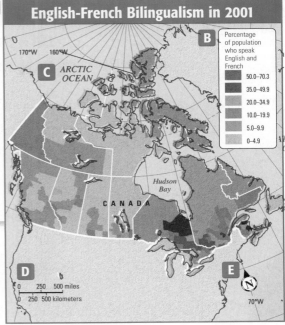

A English-French Bilingualism in 2001

B Percentage of population who speak English and French
50.0–70.3
35.0–49.9
20.0–34.9
10.0–19.9
5.0–9.9
0–4.9

170°W 160°W
C ARCTIC OCEAN
Hudson Bay
CANADA
D 0 250 500 miles / 0 250 500 kilometers
E N
70°W

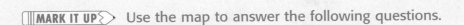

MARK IT UP Use the map to answer the following questions.

1. What does this map show? _____

_____

_____

2. In how many separate areas of Canada is more than half the population bilingual?

_____

3. Where in Canada do most of the people who speak only English live?

_____

4. Draw a straight line between the most easterly and most westerly points in Canada. About how many miles across is the country?

_____

Reading a Diagram

Diagrams combine pictures with a few words to provide a lot of information. Look at the example on the opposite page as you read each of the following strategies.

A Look at the **title** to get an idea of what the diagram is about.

B Study the **images** closely to understand each part of the diagram.

C Look at the **captions** and the **labels** for more information.

MARK IT UP Study the diagram, then answer the following questions using the strategies above.

1. What does this diagram illustrate? _____

_____

_____

2. What is one example of a composite volcano? _____

_____

_____

3. What is one difference between cinder cones and composite volcanoes?

_____

_____

4. Circle the name of the layer of the earth that lies under the continental crust.

5. Draw a box around the part of the diagram that shows the internal structure of a composite volcano.

A Volcanic Landforms

The shape and structure of a volcano are determined by the nature of its eruptions and the materials it ejects. A cinder cone, perhaps the simplest form of volcano, forms when molten lava is thrown into the air from a vent. Cinder cones, which tend to be smaller than other types of volcanoes, typically form in groups and on the sides of larger volcanoes. Composite volcanoes develop when layers of materials from successive eruptions accumulate around a vent. The diagram shows the structure of these two types of volcanoes.

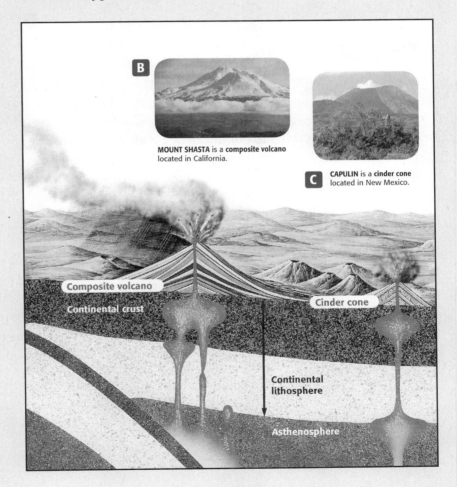

B MOUNT SHASTA is a **composite volcano** located in California.

C CAPULIN is a **cinder cone** located in New Mexico.

Composite volcano

Continental crust

Cinder cone

Continental lithosphere

Asthenosphere

Main Idea and Supporting Details

The *main idea* in a paragraph is its most important point. *Details* in the paragraph support the main idea. Identifying the main idea will help you focus on the main message the writer wants to communicate. Use the following strategies to help you identify a paragraph's main idea and supporting details.

- Look for the **main idea,** which is often the first sentence in a paragraph.

- Use the main idea to help you **summarize** the point of the paragraph.

- Identify specific **details,** including facts and examples, that support the main idea.

"Monsieur Rap"

Main idea   The French king of rap music is a rhythmic sensation called MC Solaar. Born in Senegal to parents from Chad and raised in France, he writes songs that continue to bridge cultural barriers. They weave clever French word play into

Details   American rap rhythms to communicate a global message of hope. Solaar has put his ideals into action by singing to support the release of political prisoners around the world.

MARK IT UP   Read the following paragraph. Circle the main idea. Then underline the details that support the main idea.

MC Solaar has truly become an international sensation. In 1991, he teamed up with the American rap group De la Soul at a concert in Paris. In 1992, he toured extensively through Russia and Poland and gave performances in a dozen West African countries. Three years later, after being named Best Male Singer of the Year at the 10th French "Victoires de la Musique" awards, he traveled and performed throughout France and Europe. His albums remain best-sellers in more than 20 countries.

Problem and Solution

Does the proposed solution to a problem make sense? In order to decide, you need to look at each part of the text. Use the following strategies to read the text below.

- Look at the beginning or middle of a paragraph to find the **statement of the problem.**

- Find **details** that explain the problem and tell why it is important.

- Look for the **proposed solution.**

- Identify the **supporting details** for the proposed solution.

- Think about whether the solution is a good one.

Lunchroom Language Tables Can Beef Up Students' Skills

by Tara Blum

Statement of problem

Teachers, parents, administrators, and school board members are concerned that foreign language students are not getting enough practice actually using the language in conversation.

Details about the problem

In their foreign language classes, students read dialogs from their textbooks and respond to questions, but rarely get a chance to just communicate their thoughts.

Proposed solution

One way to address this problem would be to establish language tables in the lunchroom. Students taking a specific language would eat their lunch at a designated table one day a week. The only rule would be that they must speak no English, just the foreign language.

Details about the solution

This plan has several advantages. First, it doesn't require any additional equipment or materials. Second, it wouldn't take time away from other classes or activities. Language students have to eat lunch just like everyone else. Finally, it would be a lot of fun.

Language tables would let students supplement their language skills while nourishing their bodies. And that's a recipe for success!

MARK IT UP Use the text and strategies above to answer these questions.

1. Underline the proposed solution.

2. Circle at least one reason that supports this solution.

3. Explain why you think this is or is not a good solution to the problem.

_____

_____

_____

Sequence

Sequence is the order in which events happen. Whether you read a story or a social studies lesson, it is important for you to understand *when* things happen in relation to one another. The tips below can help you identify sequence in any type of text.

- Look for the **main steps** or **events** in the sequence.

- Look for **words and phrases that signal time**, such as *in ancient times* and *today.*

- Look for **words and phrases that signal order**, such as *first, after,* and *next.*

MARK IT UP Read the passage about making cheese on the next page. Then use the information from the article and the tips above to answer the questions.

1. Underline two words or phrases that signal time.

2. Circle two words or phrases that signal order.

3. A flowchart can help you identify and understand a sequence of events. Use the information from the passage to complete this flowchart.

> **Cheese is made from milk.** The first step is _____ .

↓

> **The milk seperates into curds and whey.** Then _____ turns milk into curds and whey.

↓

> **The curds are heated and cut, and salt is added.** The curds _____ cheeses.

↓

> **The cheese is left to age.** Finally the cheese _____ .

Say Cheese

You've sliced it, diced it, melted it, spiced it—eaten it spread on crackers, over vegetables, with fruit, or by itself. You're friends with American and Swiss, and have maybe tried one of the more than 400 varieties of cheese that the French produce with pride and call *fromage*. But have you ever thought about how cheese is made?

All cheese starts with milk—from cows, goats, sheep, or other animals. In fact, if the mozzarella that tops your pizza is authentic, it came from buffaloes. According to one story, an Arab nomad accidentally made the first cheese in ancient times when the hot sun, his horse's motion, and a chemical in a saddlebag of milk turned the liquid into white lumps.

The basic cheese-making principle this Arab discovered is that milk naturally curdles, or separates into solid curds and liquid whey. The first step in helping this process along involves making the milk more acidic. This is done by adding bacteria that change the sugar in milk into lactic acid in the process of acidification.

After acidification, coagulation—turning milk into curds and whey—begins. A chemical enzyme helps the curds become solid. This enzyme occurs in rennet, which comes from the lining of calves' stomachs. Today, scientists artificially create this enzyme using yeast cells.

The curds are then heated and cut to help release any liquid that remains. Next, salt is added to improve the taste and kill unwanted bacteria, and the curds are shaped in a cheese press.

Finally, the remaining bacteria help the cheese ripen, or age. At this stage, other bacteria, like the ones that produce penicillin, may be added to help create the blue veins in bleu cheese and the white coating on Brie and Camembert. This process can take from days to decades, depending on the type of cheese being made.

So, next time you want a snack, just think about this process, smile, and say "cheese"!

A *cause* is an event that brings about another event. An *effect* is something that happens as a result of the first event. Identifying causes and effects helps you understand how events are related. Use the tips below to find causes and effects in any kind of reading.

- Look for an action or event that answers the question, "What happened?" This is the **effect.**

- Look for an action or event that answers the question, "Why did this happen?" This is the **cause.**

- Look for words or phrases that **signal** causes and effects, such as *because, as a result, therefore, consequently,* and *since.*

▐▐▐MARK IT UP⟫ Read the cause-and-effect passage on the next page. Notice that the first cause and effect are labeled. Then use the strategies above to help you answer the following questions.

1. Circle words in the passage that signal causes and effects. The first one has been done for you.

2. Some causes may have more than one effect. What are two effects of the mosquito's saliva on the body of the victim?

_____

_____

3. Complete the following diagram showing the cause and effects of mosquito bites.

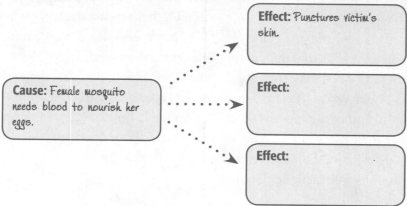

Cause: Female mosquito needs blood to nourish her eggs.

Effect: Punctures victim's skin

Effect:

Effect:

Bzz! Slap!

Cause

If you spend any time outdoors in the summer, at some point you will probably find yourself covered with mosquito bites.

Mosquitoes can transmit serious diseases such as yellow fever, encephalitis, and malaria. Usually,

Signal Word

Effect

though, mosquito bites just (cause) people to develop raised, red bumps that itch like crazy.

This is what happens. Female mosquitoes need blood to nourish the eggs developing in their bodies. Consequently, they zero in on living things whose blood they can suck. Once they find a likely victim, the attack begins.

This attack is not really a bite, since a mosquito isn't able to open her jaws. Instead, she punctures the victim's skin with sharp stylets inside her mouth. The mosquito's saliva then flows into these puncture wounds. Because the saliva keeps the victim's blood from clotting, the mosquito can drink her fill. This can sometimes amount to 150 percent of the mosquito's weight.

Meanwhile, the mosquito's saliva sets off an allergic reaction in the victim. As a result, the person develops the itchy swelling we call a mosquito bite. Ironically, if the

mosquito finishes eating before the victim slaps or drives her off, there will be less saliva left in the skin. Therefore, the allergic reaction and itching will not be so severe.

Here are some steps you can take to help prevent mosquito bites or lessen their effect if you do get bitten.

- Don't go out at prime mosquito time—from dusk to dawn.
- Use insect repellent at all times.
- If you do get bitten, DON'T SCRATCH. Scratching just increases the allergic reaction.

Comparison and Contrast

Comparing two things means showing how they are the same. *Contrasting* two things means showing how they are different. Comparisons and contrasts are important because they show how things or ideas are related. Use these tips to help you understand comparison and contrast in reading assignments such as the article on the opposite page.

- Look for **direct statements** of **comparison and contrast.** "These things are similar because…" or "One major difference is…"

- Pay attention to **words and phrases that signal comparisons,** such as *also, both, in addition to,* and *in the same way.*

- Notice **words and phrases that signal contrasts**. Some of these are *however, on the other hand, but,* and *in contrast.*

MARK IT UP Read the article on the next page. Then use the information from the article and the tips above to answer the questions.

1. Circle the words and phrases that signal comparisons. A sample has been done for you.

2. Underline the words and phrases that signal contrast. Notice the completed example.

3. A Venn diagram shows how two subjects are similar and how they are different. Complete this diagram, which uses information from the essay to compare and contrast greetings in France and America. Add one or more similarity to the center of the diagram and one or more difference to each outer circle.

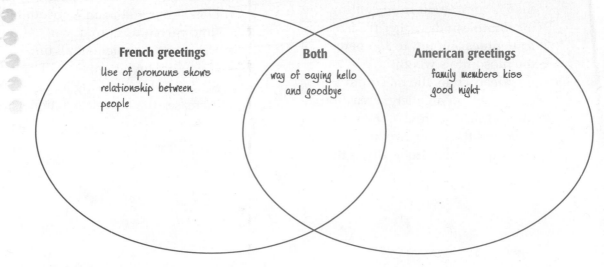

French greetings
Use of pronouns shows relationship between people

Both
way of saying hello and goodbye

American greetings
family members kiss good night

Greetings Across the Atlantic

No matter where you were born and live, you're becoming more and more a citizen of a global community. Nevertheless, differences between cultures still—and probably always will—exist. One important characteristic of a culture is how people say hello and goodbye to each other. Here's how it's done in America and a close neighbor across the ocean, France.

Comparison

In both cultures, the relationship between people determines how they greet one another. The French language includes a way of showing this relationship. In formal situations, people address each other using the pronoun *vous*. Informal and close relationships are marked by the use of *tu*. In America, the language offers no such help, Contrast such help, however, since everyone is just addressed as *you*.

American family members often kiss each other goodnight, although fathers may choose instead to shake hands with their teenage sons. To people outside the family, Americans usually offer informal greetings—a smile, a nod of the head, or a simple, "Hi, how are you?" Among teens, girlfriends also may exchange hugs, and boys, pats or punches on the arm or back.

Like Americans, the French greet family members with kisses, but not only when going to bed. They also kiss hello in the morning and when seeing each other again during the day. In addition, fathers are not as reluctant as American men to kiss their sons.

On the other hand, French people are more formal than Americans when greeting non-family-members. They shake hands and offer a formal acknowledgement with the person's title both when they meet and part. French boys also greet one another with handshakes, though they often give a girlfriend *une bise*, or several kisses on the cheeks. Teenage girls usually exchange *une bise* with both girlfriends and boyfriends.

So now you know how to give warmest greetings—in your own special way—on either side of the Atlantic!

Persuasion

To be persuasive, an opinion should be backed up with reasons and facts. After you carefully read an opinion and the reasons and facts that support it, you will be able to decide if the opinion makes sense. As you read these tips, look at the sample persuasive essay on the next page.

- Look for words or phrases that **signal an opinion**, such as *I believe, I think,* and *in my opinion.*

- Identify reasons, facts, or expert opinions that **support** the position.

- Ask yourself if the opinion and the reasons that back it up **make sense.**

- Look for **errors in reasoning,** such as overgeneralizations, that may affect the presentation of the opinion.

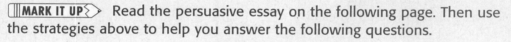 Read the persuasive essay on the following page. Then use the strategies above to help you answer the following questions.

1. Underline any words or phrases that signal the writer's opinion.

2. Circle any words or phrases that signal the opinion of persons other than the writer.

3. The writer presents both sides of this debate. List the points supporting both sides in the chart below. One reason has been provided for you.

For swimming pool	Against swimming pool
1. The school has a responsibility to teach swimming.	

Our School Needs to Get in the Swim *by Eric Legrand*

This school needs a swimming pool. Swimming is an important life skill and I believe it is the responsibility of the school to provide this essential part of students' education.

The school's mission is to educate the whole person—mind and body—and to prepare students to be productive citizens. In addition to our academic subjects, we are taught how to eat right, budget our money, and drive a car. But we don't learn the water safety skills that could someday save our lives.

The community and school board obviously don't feel the way I do, however. They repeatedly have refused to fund the building of a pool. In the opinion of one board member, "Students can take swimming lessons at the local health club." Other school officials think that the school has more important needs—repairing the sagging gym floor and installing new lockers, for example.

In my opinion, these reasons are not valid. First, most students cannot afford lessons at the health club. Even those who have the money don't have the time. They're busy with homework and other activities during the school year and have to work or go to summer school during vacation.

I agree that the gym floor should be replaced and wouldn't mind having a new locker. But I believe that the educational needs of the students should come first. Swimming is one of the best forms of exercise there is. Even if knowing how to swim never saves your life, it can improve its quality. Isn't that what an education is all about?

Social studies class becomes easier when you understand how your textbook's words, pictures, and maps work together to give you information. Following these tips can make you a better reader of social studies lessons. As you read the tips, look at the sample lesson on the right-hand page.

A Read the **title** of the lesson and other **headings** to find out what the lesson is about. Smaller headings may introduce subtopics that are related to the main topic.

B Read the **main ideas** or **objectives** listed on the first page of the lesson. These items summarize the lesson and help set a purpose for your reading.

C Look at the **vocabulary terms** listed on the lesson's first page. These terms will be boldfaced or underlined where they appear in the text.

D Notice **how information is organized.** In social studies lessons, ideas are often presented using sequence, cause and effect, comparison and contrast, and main idea and supporting details.

E Carefully examine **visual features** such as photographs, boxed text, maps, charts, bulleted lists, time lines, diagrams, and information in the margins. Think about how the visuals and the text are related.

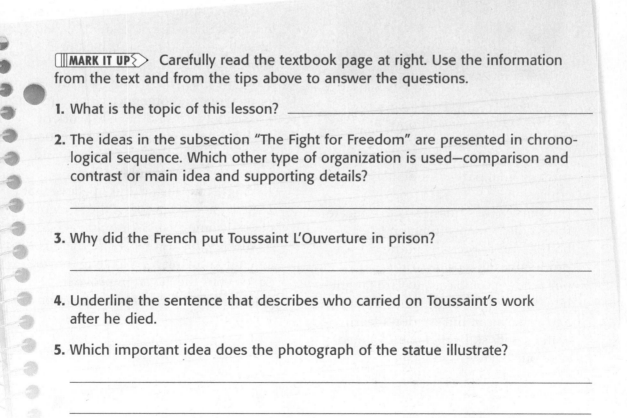

MARK IT UP Carefully read the textbook page at right. Use the information from the text and from the tips above to answer the questions.

1. What is the topic of this lesson? _____

2. The ideas in the subsection "The Fight for Freedom" are presented in chrono-logical sequence. Which other type of organization is used—comparison and contrast or main idea and supporting details?

   _____

3. Why did the French put Toussaint L'Ouverture in prison?

   _____

4. Underline the sentence that describes who carried on Toussaint's work after he died.

5. Which important idea does the photograph of the statue illustrate?

   _____

   _____

Latin American Peoples Win Independence

TERMS & NAMES **C**
- *peninsulares*
- creoles
- mulattos
- Simón Bolívar
- José de San Martín
- Miguel Hidalgo
- José Morelos

MAIN IDEA

Spurred by discontent and Enlightenment ideas, peoples in Latin America fought colonial rule.

WHY IT MATTERS NOW

Sixteen of today's Latin American nations gained their independence at this time.

SETTING THE STAGE By the late 1700s, the Americas, already troubled by Enlightenment ideas, were electrified by the news of the French Revolution. The French ideals of liberty, equality, and fraternity inspired many Latin Americans to rise up against their French, Spanish, and Portuguese masters.

Revolution in Haiti

The French colony called Saint Domingue was the first Latin American territory to free itself from European rule. Saint Domingue, now known as Haiti, occupied the western third of the island of Hispaniola in the Caribbean Sea.

Background
About 35,000 Europeans stood at the top of the social ladder in Haiti in the late 1700s. They were mainly French.

Nearly 500,000 enslaved Africans—the vast majority of Saint Domingue's population—lived at the bottom of the social system. Most slaves worked on plantations, and they outnumbered their masters dramatically. White masters thus used brutal methods to terrorize slaves and keep them powerless.

D **The Fight for Freedom** The slaves soon showed that, in fact, they were not powerless. In August 1791, an African priest named Boukman raised a call for revolution. Within a few days, 100,000 slaves rose in revolt. A leader soon emerged, Toussaint L'Ouverture (too-SAN loo-vair-TOOR), an ex-slave. Toussaint was untrained in the military and in diplomacy. Even so, he rose to become a skilled general and diplomat. It is said that he got the name L'Ouverture ("opening" in French) because he was so skilled at finding openings in the enemy lines. By 1801, Toussaint had moved into Spanish Santo Domingo (the eastern two-thirds of Hispaniola). He took control of the territory and freed the slaves.

In January 1802, 16,000 French troops landed in Saint Domingue to depose Toussaint. In May, Toussaint agreed to halt the revolution if the French would end slavery. Despite the agreement, the French soon accused him of planning another uprising. They seized him and sent him to a prison in the French Alps. In that cold mountain jail, he died 10 months later, in April 1803.

Background
By 1600, almost the entire Arawak population had disappeared because of European conquest, warfare, disease, or slavery.

Haiti's Independence Toussaint's general, Jean-Jacques Dessalines (zhahn-ZHAHK day-sah-LEEN), took up the fight for freedom where Toussaint had left off. On January 1, 1804, General Dessalines declared the colony an independent country. It was the first black colony to free itself from European control. He called the country Haiti, which meant "mountainous land" in the language of the native Arawak inhabitants of the island.

E

J.J.DESSALINES
Kaiser auf St. Domingo.

Reading a science textbook becomes easier when you understand how the explanations, drawings, and special terms work together. Use the strategies below to help you better understand your science textbook. Look at the examples on the opposite page as you read each strategy in this list.

A Preview the **title** and any **headings** to see what scientific concepts you will learn about.

B Read the **key ideas** or **objectives.** These items summarize the lesson and help set a purpose for your reading.

C Read the list of **vocabulary terms** that will be introduced and defined in the lesson.

D Notice the **boldfaced** and *italicized* terms in the text. Look for the definitions of these terms.

E Carefully examine any **pictures** or **diagrams.** Read the **captions** to see how the graphics help to illustrate the text.

MARK IT UP Use the strategies above and the science lesson on the next page to answer these questions.

1. Underline the title of the lesson.

2. Circle the list of vocabulary words that will appear in the lesson.

3. Draw a box around one boldfaced term in the lesson.

4. Examine the graph and read the text directly above it. What idea does the graph illustrate?

_____

_____

5. At what latitude is the elevation of the snow line lowest?

_____

_____

15.1

B KEY IDEAS

Glaciers are huge ice masses that move under the influence of gravity.

Glaciers form from compacted and recrystallized snow.

C KEY VOCABULARY
- glacier
- snow line
- firn
- valley glacier
- continental glacier
- ice cap

A ## What Is a Glacier?

About 75 percent of Earth's fresh water is frozen in glaciers. A **glacier** is a large mass of compacted snow and ice that moves under the force of gravity. A glacier changes Earth's surface as it erodes geological features in one place and then redeposits the material elsewhere thus altering the landscape.

Where Glaciers Form

Glaciers form in areas that are always covered by snow. In such areas, more snow falls than melts each year; as a result layers of snow build up from previous years. Climates cold enough to cause such conditions may be found in any part of the world. Air temperatures drop as you climb high above sea level and as you travel farther from the equator.

Even in equatorial areas, however, a layer of permanent snow may exist on high mountains at high elevation. Farther from the equator, the elevation need not be so high for a layer of permanent snow to exist. In the polar areas, permanent snow may be found even at sea level. The lowest elevation at which the layer of permanent snow occurs in summer is called **D** the **snow line.** If a mountain is completely covered with snow in winter but without snow in summer, it has no snow line.

In general, the snow line occurs at lower and lower elevations as the latitudes approach the poles. The snow line also changes according to total yearly snowfall and the amount of solar exposure. Thus, the elevation of the snow line is not the same for all places at a given latitude.

VISUALIZATIONS
CLASSZONE.COM

Examine seasonal migration of snow cover.
Keycode: ES1501

E

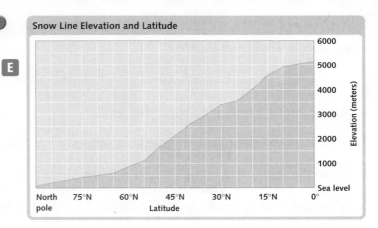

Snow Line Elevation and Latitude

VOCABULARY STRATEGY

The word *firn* comes from a German word meaning "last year's snow." The word *névé* is related to a Latin word meaning "cooled by snow."

How Glaciers Form

Except for bare rock cliffs, a mountain above the snow line is always buried in snow. Great basins below the highest peaks are filled with snow that can be hundreds of meters thick. In these huge snowfields, buried snow becomes compressed and recrystallizes into a rough, granular ice material called **firn** (feern) or névé (nay-VAY).

318   **Unit 4** Earth's Changing Surface

Mathematics

Reading in mathematics is different from reading in history, literature, or science. A math lesson has few words, but instead illustrates math concepts using numbers, symbols, formulas, equations, diagrams, and word problems. Use the following strategies, and the lesson on the next page, to help you better understand your math textbook.

A Scan the **title** and **headings** to see which math concepts you will learn about.

B Look for **goals, objectives** or **key ideas**. These help focus your reading.

C Read **explanations** carefully. Sometimes a concept is explained in more than one way to make sure you understand it.

D Look for **special features** such as study or technology tips or connections to real life. These provide more help or information.

E Study any **worked-out solutions** to sample problems. These are the key to understanding how to do the homework assignment.

|MARK IT UP⟩ Use the strategies above and the mathematics lesson on the next page to answer these questions.

1. What is this lesson about? _____

_____

2. Put a star next to the goals of the lesson.

3. Underline the definition of scientific notation.

4. Circle the explanations of how to rewrite numbers in decimal form.

5. What practical application does scientific notation have in the real world?

_____

_____

Scientific Notation

GOAL 1   USING SCIENTIFIC NOTATION

B *What you should learn*

GOAL 1 Use scientific notation to represent numbers.

GOAL 2 Use scientific notation to describe **real-life** situations, such as the price per acre of the Alaska purchase in **Example 6**.

D *Why you should learn it*

▼ To solve **real-life** problems, such as finding the amount of water discharged by the Amazon River each year in **Example 5**.

A number is written in **scientific notation** if it is of the form $c \times 10^n$, where $1 \le c < 10$ and n is an integer. **C**

▶ ACTIVITY

Developing Concepts

Investigating Scientific Notation

1 Rewrite each number in decimal form.

  a. 6.43×10^4 **b.** 3.072×10^6 **c.** 4.2×10^{-2} **d.** 1.52×10^{-3}

2 Describe a general rule for writing the decimal form of a number given in scientific notation. How many places do you move the decimal point? Do you move the decimal point left or right?

EXAMPLE 1   *Rewriting in Decimal Form*

Rewrite in decimal form.

  a. 2.834×10^2 **b.** 4.9×10^5 **c.** 7.8×10^{-1} **d.** 1.23×10^{-6}

SOLUTION **E**

  a. $2.834 \times 10^2 = 283.4$ Move decimal point right 2 places.

  b. $4.9 \times 10^5 = 490,000$ Move decimal point right 5 places.

  c. $7.8 \times 10^{-1} = 0.78$ Move decimal point left 1 place.

  d. $1.23 \times 10^{-6} = 0.00000123$ Move decimal point left 6 places.

EXAMPLE 2   *Rewriting in Scientific Notation*

  a. $34,690 = 3.469 \times 10^4$ Move decimal point left 4 places.

  b. $1.78 = 1.78 \times 10^0$ Move decimal point 0 places.

  c. $0.039 = 3.9 \times 10^{-2}$ Move decimal point right 2 places.

  d. $0.000722 = 7.22 \times 10^{-4}$ Move decimal point right 4 places.

  e. $5,600,000,000 = 5.6 \times 10^9$ Move decimal point left 9 places.

470   **Chapter 8** *Exponents and Exponential Functions*

To get a part-time job or to register for summer camp or classes at the local community center, you will have to fill out an application. Being able to understand the format of an application will help you fill it out correctly. Use the following strategies and the sample on the next page to help you understand any application.

A **Begin at the top.** Scan the application to understand the different sections.

B Look for special **instructions for filling out** the application.

C Note any **request for materials** or **special information** that must be included with the application.

D Watch for **sections you don't have to fill in** or **questions you don't have to answer.**

E Look for **difficult or confusing words** or abbreviations. Look them up in a dictionary or ask someone what they mean.

MARK IT UP Use the warranty application on the following page and the strategies above to answer the questions.

1. Why is it important to fill out and mail this warranty application?

_____

_____

2. Underline the phrase that tells when the application must be mailed.

3. What information about the product do you have to supply?

_____

4. Circle the part of the application that you do not have to fill out.

5. What purchase document must you use to fill out this application?

_____

6. ASSESSMENT PRACTICE Circle the letter of the correct answer.
What amount should you include in the box marked "retail price paid"?
A. the total amount you paid for the product
B. the total amount you paid minus the cost of the maintenance agreement
C. the price marked on the product
D. the cost of extra charges, such as delivery and installation

A Congratulations on investing in a Morel product. Your decision will reward you for years to come. Please complete your Warranty Registration Card to ensure that you receive all the privileges and protection that come with your purchase.

Your completed Warranty Registration Card serves as confirmation of ownership in the event of theft.

Returning the attached card guarantees you'll receive all the special offers for which your purchase makes you eligible.

DETACH AND MAIL PORTION BELOW.

USA Limited Warranty Registration	
123456 XXXX	**ABCDEFG7654321**
MODEL NUMBER	SERIAL NUMBER

Registering your product ensures that you receive all of the benefits you are entitled to as a Morel customer. Complete the information below in ink, and drop this card in the nearest mailbox.

B **IMPORTANT - RETURN WITHIN TEN DAYS**

Date of Purchase

Your Name
First | Initial | Last

Address
Street | Apt. #
City | State | ZIP Code

C **Retail Price Paid $** _____ **.00**
(Excluding sales tax, maintenance agreement, delivery, installation, and trade-in allowance.) **E**

D **Your Phone Number** (optional)
Area Code | Phone Number

MOREL

When you research information for a report or project, you may use the World Wide Web. Once you find the site you want, the strategies below will help you find the facts and details you need. Look at the sample Web page on the right as you read each of the strategies.

A Notice the page's **Web address,** or URL. Write down the Web address or bookmark it if you think you might return to the page at another time or if you need to add it to a list of sources.

B Read the **title** of the page. The title usually tells you what topics the page covers.

C Look for **menu bars** along the top, bottom, or side of the page. These guide you to other parts of the site that may be useful.

D Notice any **links** to other parts of the site or to related pages. Links are often highlighted in color or underlined.

E Many sites have a link that allows you to **contact** the creators with questions or feedback.

F Use a **search feature** to find out quickly whether the information you want to locate appears anywhere on the site.

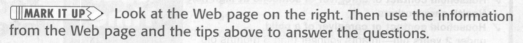 **MARK IT UP** Look at the Web page on the right. Then use the information from the Web page and the tips above to answer the questions.

1. Circle the Web address of this site.

2. Draw boxes around two places you can search the site to see if it contains the information you need.

3. What is the name of the president of QN? _____

4. Put a star by the link you should click on to make an online contribution to QN.

5. ASSESSMENT PRACTICE Circle the letter of the best answer.
This site is designed to give information about
A. issues of interest to people in Quebec
B. education in Quebec
C. raising children in Quebec
D. politicians people in Quebec should vote for

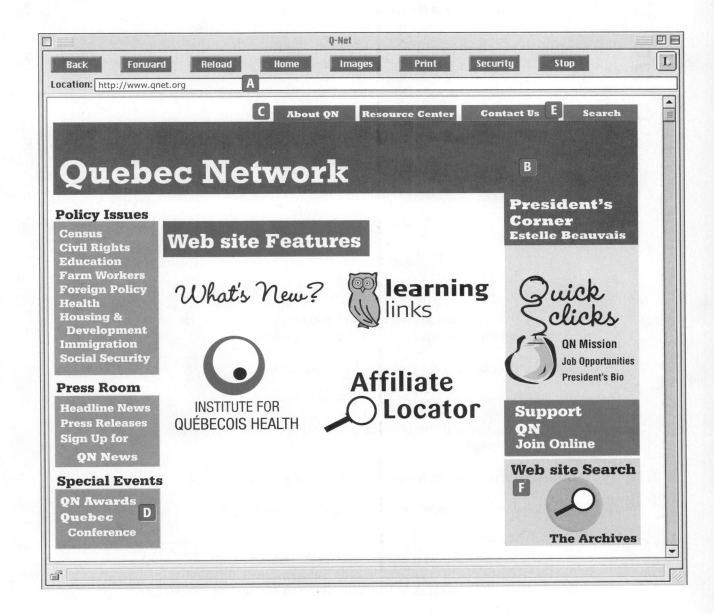

Q-Net

Back | Forward | Reload | Home | Images | Print | Security | Stop

L

Location: http://www.qnet.org **A**

C About QN | Resource Center | Contact Us **E** | Search

Quebec Network

B

Policy Issues

Census
Civil Rights
Education
Farm Workers
Foreign Policy
Health
Housing &
   Development
Immigration
Social Security

Press Room

Headline News
Press Releases
Sign Up for
   QN News

Special Events

QN Awards
Quebec
   Conference **D**

Web site Features

What's New?

learning links

INSTITUTE FOR
QUÉBECOIS HEALTH

Affiliate
Locator

President's Corner
Estelle Beauvais

Quick clicks

QN Mission
Job Opportunities
President's Bio

Support QN
Join Online

Web site Search
F

The Archives

Reading Technical Directions

Reading technical directions will help you understand how to use the products you buy. Use the following tips to help you read a variety of technical directions.

A Look carefully at any **diagrams** or **other images** of the product.

B **Read all the directions** carefully at least once before using the product.

C Notice **headings** or **lines** that separate one section from another.

D Look for **numbers, letters,** or **bullets** that give the steps in sequence.

E Watch for **warnings** or **notes** with more information.

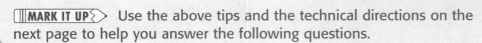 Use the above tips and the technical directions on the next page to help you answer the following questions.

1. What kind of battery do you need for the clock?

_____

2. How do you know if the time displayed is AM or PM? Circle the answer on the next page.

3. Underline the steps to follow in setting the alarm.

4. How long will the alarm sound if you don't turn it off?

_____

5. **ASSESSMENT PRACTICE** Circle the letter of the correct answer.
Which of the following is NOT a safe place to set up the clock radio?
A. on a stable, flat desk
B. in the bathroom
C. away from open windows
D. on a bedside table

Alarm Clock Radio
INSTRUCTIONS FOR USE

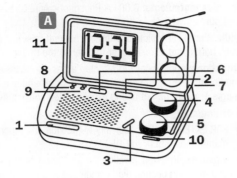

1. SNOOZE/LIGHT BUTTON
2. FUNCTION SWITCH
3. BAND SWITCH
4. TUNING CONTROL
5. VOLUME CONTROL
6. TIME/ALARM SET SWITCH
7. BATTERY DOOR (RADIO)
8. HOUR BUTTON
9. MINUTE BUTTON
10. EJECT BUTTON
11. BATTERY HOLDER (CLOCK)

BATTERIES
FOR RADIO:
To insert batteries, remove the BATTERY DOOR (7) and insert 2 AAA batteries, observing the correct position of the polarity.

FOR CLOCK:
Pull out the BATTERY HOLDER (11). Use a 1.5 volt battery and place with positive electrode facing front. Reinsert battery holder.

C **HOW TO PLAY THE RADIO**
- Press the EJECT BUTTON (10) to open lid.
- Turn the FUNCTION SWITCH (2) TO "ON" position.
- Use the BAND SWITCH (3) to select broadcasting band (AM or FM).
- Turn the TUNING CONTROL knob (4) to select the listening station.

D **TO SET THE TIME**
- Slide the TIME/ALARM SET SWITCH (6) to the "T.SET" position.
- Depress the HOUR BUTTON (8) until the correct hour is displayed. Be careful to set time to AM or PM as required. When PM time is registered, a "P" will apppear on the display.
- Depress the MINUTE BUTTON (9) until the correct minute is reached.

TO SET THE ALARM
- Slide the TIME/ALARM SET SWITCH (6) to the "AL.SET" position. "AL" indicator will appear on the display.
- Depress the HOUR BUTTON (8) until the desired alarm hour is displayed. Be careful to correctly set alarm to AM or PM as required. When PM time is registered, a "P" will appear on the display.
- Depress the MINUTE BUTTON (9) until the desired alarm time is reached.

WAKE TO ALARM
- Set the FUNCTION SWITCH (2) TO "ALARM" position. When the desired alarm time is reached, you will hear a sequential "BEEP" alarm for 60 seconds.
- To shut the alarm off temporarily, press the SNOOZE/LIGHT BUTTON (1) once. The alarm will stop for 4 minutes, then come on again.
- To stop the alarm completely, set the FUNCTION SWITCH (2) to "OFF" position.

WAKE TO MUSIC
- Set the FUNCTION SWITCH (2) TO "AUTO" position.
- The radio will turn on automatically at your desired alarm time.

SAFETY PRECAUTIONS **E**
- Do not place the unit near a moisture environment, such as a bathtub, kitchen, sink, etc. The unit should be well protected from rain, dew, condensation, or any form of dampness.
- Do not place the unit on surfaces with strong vibration. Place the unit only on flat, stable, and level surfaces.

Product Information: Directions for Use

Many of the products you buy come with instructions that tell you how to use them correctly. Directions for use may appear on the product itself, on its packaging, or on a separate insert. Learning to read and follow directions for use is important for your safety. As you read each strategy below, look at the sample.

A Read any **headings** to find out what kinds of information are given with the product.

B Read the **directions**, which usually tell you *why, how, when,* and *where* to use the product, *how much to use, how often,* and *when* to stop using it.

C Carefully read any **warnings** given with the product. The manufacturer will usually tell you what to do if you experience any problems.

D Look for any **contact information** that tells you where to call or write if you have a question about the product.

Solution of Hydrogen Peroxide 3% U.S.P.

Active ingredient: Hydrogen peroxide 3%

Inactive ingredients: 0.001% Phosphoric Acid as a stabilizer and purified water

Indications: For topical use to help prevent infection in minor cuts, burns, and abrasions, or to cleanse the mouth.

Directions: Apply locally to affected areas. To cleanse the mouth, dilute with an equal amount of water and use as a gargle or rinse. Do not use in excess of ten consecutive days.

Warnings:

- FOR EXTERNAL USE: Topically to the skin and mucous membranes. KEEP OUT OF EYES.
- If redness, irritation, swelling, or pain persists or increases or if infection occurs, discontinue use and consult a physician.
- KEEP THIS AND ALL DRUGS OUT OF THE REACH OF CHILDREN. **In case of accidental ingestion, seek professional assistance or contact a Poison Control Center immediately**.

Storage: Keep bottle tightly closed and at controlled room temperature 59°–86° F (15°–30° C). Do not shake bottle.

Questions? (888) 555-1234

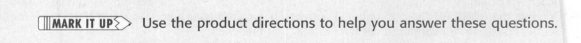 Use the product directions to help you answer these questions.

1. How do you use the product to cleanse your mouth? _____

_____

2. Circle the active ingredient in this product.

3. What should you do if someone accidentally swallows this product? Underline the answer.

4. Draw a box around the number you should call if you have questions about the product.

5. **ASSESSMENT PRACTICE** Circle the letter of the correct answer.
   When should you stop using this product?
   A. when the temperature drops below 59° F
   B. if pain and swelling increase
   C. if you have a minor abrasion
   D. ten days after you buy it

Reading a Bus Schedule

Knowing how to read a bus schedule accurately can help you get where you need to go–on time. Look at the sample bus schedule as you read the tips below.

A Look at the **title** to know what the schedule covers.

B Identify **labels** that show **dates** or **days of the week** to help you understand how the daily or weekly schedule works.

C Look at **place labels** to know what stops are listed on the schedule.

D Look for **expressions of time** to know what hours or minutes are listed on the schedule.

E Pay attention to the **organization** of the information. Read across the row to see when a bus will reach each location.

A Route 238   Quincy Center Station - Holbrook/Randolph Commuter Rail Station via Crawford Sq.

WEEKDAY MORNINGS **B**

C Leave Quincy Station	Leave S. Shore Plaza	Leave Crawford Square	Arrive Holb./Rand. Commuter Rail Sta.	Leave Holb./Rand. Commuter Rail Sta.	Leave Crawford Square	Leave S. Shore Plaza	Arrive Quincy Station
D 5:25A	5:43A	5:58A	...	6:25A	6:29A	6:42A	7:08A
6:10	6:28	6:43	6:47A	6:50	6:54	7:07	7:35
6:25	6:43	6:58	7:03	7:20	7:25	7:38	8:06
6:45	7:03	7:19	7:24	7:50	7:55	8:08	8:36
7:05	7:25	7:41	7:46	8:25	8:30	8:43	9:11 **E**
7:30	7:50	8:06	8:11	8:55	9:00	9:13	9:41
7:55	8:15	8:31	8:36	9:25	9:30	9:46	10:14
8:15	8:35	8:51	8:56	10:05	10:10	10:26	10:54
9:10	9:30	9:46	9:51	11:00	11:05	11:21	11:49
10:05	10:25	10:41	10:46				
10:55	11:15	11:31	11:36				

MARK IT UP Use the bus schedule and the strategies on this page to answer the following questions.

1. Circle the name of one stop on this route.

_____

_____

2. What time does the last bus leave Quincy Station for Holb./Rand. Commuter Rail Station on weekday mornings?

_____

3. If you took the 7:25 AM bus from Crawford Square, when would you arrive at Quincy Station?

4. ASSESSMENT PRACTICE Circle the letter of the correct answer. If you have a 10:15 meeting at S. Shore Plaza on Tuesday, what's the latest bus you can take from Holb./Rand. Commuter Rail Station?

A. 8:25   **B.** 8:55   **C.** 9:25   **D.** 10:05

Test Preparation Strategies

In this section you'll find strategies and practice to help you with many different kinds of standardized tests. The strategies apply to questions based on long and short readings, as well as questions about charts, graphs, and product labels. You'll also find examples and practice for revising-and-editing tests and writing tests. Applying the strategies to the practice materials and thinking through the answers will help you succeed in many formal testing situations.

Test Preparation Strategies

You can prepare for tests in several ways. First, study and understand the content that will be on the test. Second, learn as many test-taking techniques as you can. These techniques will help you better understand the questions and how to answer them. Following are some general suggestions for preparing for and taking tests. Starting on page 206, you'll find more detailed suggestions and test-taking practice.

Successful Test Taking

 Study Content Throughout the Year

1. **Master the content of your class.** The best way to study for tests is to read, understand, and review the content of your class. Read your daily assignments carefully. Study the notes that you have taken in class. Participate in class discussions. Work with classmates in small groups to help one another learn. You might trade writing assignments and comment on your classmates' work.

2. **Use your textbook for practice.** Your textbook includes many different types of questions. Some may ask you to talk about a story you just read. Others may ask you to figure out what's wrong with a sentence or how to make a paragraph sound better. Try answering these questions out loud and in writing. This type of practice can make taking a test much easier.

3. **Learn how to understand the information in charts, maps, and graphic organizers.** One type of test question may ask you to look at a graphic organizer, such as a spider map, and explain something about the information you see there. Another type of question may ask you to look at a map to find a particular place. You'll find charts, maps, and graphic organizers to study in your textbook. You'll also find charts, maps, and graphs in your science, mathematics, literature, and social studies textbooks. When you look at these, ask yourself, What information is being presented and why is it important?

4. **Practice taking tests.** Use copies of tests you have taken in the past or in other classes for practice. Every test has a time limit, so set a timer for 15 or 20 minutes and then begin your practice. Try to finish the test in the time you've given yourself.

☑ Reading Check In what practical way can your textbook help you prepare for a test?

5. Talk about test-taking experiences. After you've taken a classroom test or quiz, talk about it with your teacher and classmates. Which types of questions were the hardest to understand? What made them difficult? Which questions seemed easiest, and why? When you share test-taking techniques with your classmates, everyone can become a successful test taker.

 ## Use Strategies During the Test

1. Read the directions carefully. You can't be a successful test taker unless you know exactly what you are expected to do. Look for key words and phrases, such as *circle the best answer, write a paragraph,* or *choose the word that best completes each sentence.*

2. Learn how to read test questions. Test questions can sometimes be difficult to figure out. They may include unfamiliar language or be written in an unfamiliar way. Try rephrasing the question in a simpler way using words you understand. Always ask yourself, What type of information does this question want me to provide?

3. Pay special attention when using a separate answer sheet. If you accidentally skip a line on an answer sheet, all the rest of your answers may be wrong! Try one or more of the following techniques:

- Use a ruler on the answer sheet to make sure you are placing your answers on the correct line.

- After every five answers, check to make sure you're on the right line.

- Each time you turn a page of the test booklet, check to make sure the number of the question is the same as the number of the answer line on the answer sheet.

- If the answer sheet has circles, fill them in neatly. A stray pencil mark might cause the scoring machine to count the answer as incorrect.

4. If you're not sure of the answer, make your best guess. Unless you've been told that there is a penalty for guessing, choose the answer that you think is likeliest to be correct.

5. Keep track of the time. Answering all the questions on a test usually results in a better score. That's why finishing the test is important. Keep track of the time you have left. At the beginning of the test, figure out how many questions you will have to answer by the halfway point in order to finish in the time given.

☑ **Reading Check** What are at least two good ways to avoid skipping lines on an answer sheet?

Understand Types of Test Questions

Most tests include two types of questions: multiple choice and open-ended. Specific strategies will help you understand and correctly answer each type of question.

A **multiple-choice question** has two parts. The first part is the question itself, called the stem. The second part is a series of possible answers. Usually four possible answers are provided, and only one of them is correct. Your task is to choose the correct answer. Here are some strategies to help you do just that.

1. Read and think about each question carefully before looking at the possible answers.

2. Pay close attention to key words in the question. For example, look for the word *not*, as in "Which of the following is not a cause of the conflict in this story?"

3. Read and think about all of the possible answers before making your choice.

4. Reduce the number of choices by eliminating any answers you know are incorrect. Then, think about why some of the remaining choices might also be incorrect.

   - If two of the choices are pretty much the same, both are probably wrong.

   - Answers that contain any of the following words are usually incorrect: *always, never, none, all,* and *only.*

5. If you're still unsure about an answer, see if any of the following applies:

   - When one choice is longer and more detailed than the others, it is often the correct answer.

   - When a choice repeats a word that is in the question, it may be the correct answer.

   - When two choices are direct opposites, one of them is likely the correct answer.

   - When one choice includes one or more of the other choices, it is often the correct answer.

   - When a choice includes the word *some* or *often*, it may be the correct answer.

   - If one of the choices is *All of the above*, make sure that at least two of the other choices seem correct.

   - If one of the choices is *None of the above*, make sure that none of the other choices seems correct.

An **open-ended test item** can take many forms. It might ask you

☑ Reading Check What words in a multiple-choice question probably signal a wrong answer?

to write a word or phrase to complete a sentence. You might be asked to create a chart, draw a map, or fill in a graphic organizer. Sometimes, you will be asked to write one or more paragraphs in response to a writing prompt. Use the following strategies when reading and answering open-ended items:

1. If the item includes directions, read them carefully. Take note of any steps required.

2. Look for key words and phrases in the item as you plan how you will respond. Does the item ask you to identify a cause-and-effect relationship or to compare and contrast two or more things? Are you supposed to provide a sequence of events or make a generalization? Does the item ask you to write an essay in which you state your point of view and then try to persuade others that your view is correct?

3. If you're going to be writing a paragraph or more, plan your answer. Jot down notes and a brief outline of what you want to say before you begin writing.

4. Focus your answer. Don't include everything you can think of, but be sure to include everything the item asks for.

5. If you're creating a chart or drawing a map, make sure your work is as clear as possible.

☑ **Reading Check** What are at least three key strategies for answering an open-ended question?

Reading Test Model
LONG SELECTIONS

DIRECTIONS Following is a selection about the French king Louis XIV, "The Sun King." Read the passage carefully. The notes in the side columns will help you prepare for the types of questions that are likely to follow a reading like this. You might want to preview the questions on pages 135–136 before you begin reading.

The Sun King

It was 1643. King Louis XIII had just died, and his five-year-old son ascended the throne. Over the next 54 years, Louis XIV would become the most powerful ruler in France's history. Because he believed that all power radiated from him, he was called the Sun King. In fact, he thought he and France were one. *"L'état, c'est moi,"* (I am the state) he boasted.

Mazarin Rules No five year old, even the Sun King himself, was capable of running a country, however. The true ruler of France during the boy's youth was the prime minister, Cardinal Mazarin. By ending the Thirty Years' War, Mazarin made France the most powerful country in Europe. He lost support at home, though, by strengthening the central government and raising taxes.

These domestic policies affected the French nobles particularly, and they rebelled. They rioted throughout the country and threatened the young king's life. As a result, Louis vowed to become so strong that no one could threaten him again.

READING STRATEGIES FOR ASSESSMENT

Look for the main idea of the article. What does the author want you to learn about and remember when you have finished reading?

Identify causes and effects. How did rebellions by the nobles affect the young Louis? Why?

Discovering French, Nouveau! Level 1

Louis Takes Over Louis got his chance when Mazarin died in 1661. He was still only 23 years old, but knew his own mind. "The scene has changed," he proclaimed. He decided to rule without a prime minister and immersed himself in every detail of the government—from the food that was served at his table to the movement of his troops on the battlefield. He described his view of his role in a letter to his son:

> *In a well-run state, all eyes are fixed upon the monarch alone. . . . Nothing is undertaken, nothing is expected, nothing is done except through him alone.*

Pay attention to passages set off from the text. This indented passage is a quotation from Louis XIV. What does it tell you about his role as king?

Not surprisingly, one of his first acts was to bar the nobles from his councils. This weakened their power and brought the government more under the direct control of the king. Louis also gave more power to the government agents who collected taxes and administered justice—and who reported directly to him.

The Economy Booms Although Louis held the reins of government tightly, he did rely on advisers in certain areas. His minister of finance, Jean-Baptiste Colbert, led the way in directing France's economic growth. Colbert tried to keep money in the country by building France's manufacturing industries. He did this by giving money and tax breaks to manufacturers and by putting high taxes on imported goods. Under Colbert's guidance,

Note supporting details. What actions did Colbert take to support France's manufacturing industries?

Louis encouraged his subjects to migrate to the French colony in Canada. There, they could bolster the economy by trading in furs.

The King Lives Well Louis XIV did everything on a grand scale. Although he was only 5 feet 5 inches tall, he seemed much taller because he had excellent posture and held himself with dignity. The high-heeled shoes that he often wore also helped.

The king surrounded himself with luxury. He had a staff of nearly 500 cooks, waiters, and other servants just to keep him well fed. At one meal, he reportedly ate four servings of soup, a whole pheasant, a partridge in garlic sauce, two slices of ham, hard-boiled eggs, a salad, a dish of pastries, and fruit. With an appetite like that, it's a wonder he wasn't as wide as he was tall!

To make sure the nobles did not rebel against him as they had done when he was a child, Louis kept hundreds of them at his palace. They competed to have the honor of waiting outside his bedroom and of being one of the four privileged to help him dress. While away from their homes, the nobles also had less influence over the people—increasing the king's power even more.

Culture Flourishes If Louis XIV was the sun around which all France revolved, the palace he had built at Versailles was its shining glory. It stretches for about 500

Focus on topic sentences. Usually the first sentence of a paragraph, a topic sentence tells you what the paragraph is about.

yards, has approximately 2,000 rooms, and is surrounded by 15,000 acres of woods and gardens dotted with 1,400 fountains. A huge statue of the king looks over the massive courtyard. One of the palace's most magnificent rooms is the Hall of Mirrors. Around about 240 feet long and 40 feet high, it has 17 gigantic windows that look out on the garden. A mirror directly across from each window reflects the view and makes the room seem twice as large. The palace was a showcase for the king's wealth and power and made him the envy of all Europe.

Draw conclusions. What does this information suggest about Louis XIV's character?

Louis used the palace as a showcase for other arts, especially ballet and opera. Not content to be just a patron, he also participated, actually dancing the title role in the ballet *The Sun King*.

Louis Wages War To keep France the most powerful European state, Louis XIV waged many wars to gain territory from Spain and England. The French people suffered greatly as a result, both in taxes to support the army and in lives lost in battle.

Make predictions. How do you think the French people would react to their suffering under Louis XIV?

In 1700, the king of Spain died, leaving Spain's throne to Louis's 17-year-old grandson, Philip. This effectively united France and Spain, the two greatest European states. Much of Europe banded together to oppose these two countries in the 12-year War of the Spanish Succession. The war finally ended with a treaty that left Philip as king of

Spain, but kept France and Spain as separate monarchies.

Realizing that his wars and extravagant spending had almost ruined France, Louis XIV died, sad and sorry, in 1715. The Sun King was gone, but the French people would soon rise from the darkness in a revolution that would change the world.

Now answer questions 1–6. Base your answers on the selection "The Sun King." Then check yourself by reading through the Answer Strategies in the side columns.

1 Which pair of words best describes Louis XIV?

   A. artistic and shy

   B. generous and self-confident

   C. strong and vain

   D. aggressive and thrifty

> **Read the answers carefully.** Some answers include one word that describes King Louis XIV. Look for the answer in which both words describe him.

2 Which of the following statements best expresses the main idea of this selection?

   A. Louis XIV totally identified with France and was its most powerful ruler.

   B. Louis destroyed the country by his lavish lifestyle and costly wars.

   C. Under the Sun King's rule, France's economy and arts blossomed.

   D. Louis XIV became a great king to make up for being very short.

> **Look for the main idea.** Remember that the main idea of the selection expresses the point of the whole passage, not just part of it.

3 What is the primary reason that Louis built his magnificent palace at Versailles?

   A. to keep the nobles occupied so they wouldn't interfere in the government

   B. to provide employment for French bricklayers, gardeners, servants, and cooks

   C. to keep French money in the French economy

   D. to show off his wealth and success to the other heads of Europe

> **Reread the selection.** In this case, all the answers are mentioned in the passage about Versailles. Reread it to determine which reason was the most important.

Pay attention to key words. The key word in this question is *not*. Three of the answers did influence Louis. Choose the one that either was not a motivation or was not mentioned in the selection.

4 Which of the following did NOT motivate Louis to become an all-powerful king?

A. his inner strength and confidence

B. rebellions by the nobles when he was young

C. his father's weakness

D. the belief that a successful state required a powerful ruler

Don't rely on your memory. All of these answers may sound familiar, because each is discussed somewhere in the selection. Only one relates to Louis's wars, though. Skim the section "Louis Wages War" before responding.

5 What effect did Louis XIV's wars have on the French people?

A. They angered the nobles and led to widespread riots.

B. They left many dead and burdened the survivors with heavy taxes.

C. They caused many citizens to immigrate to Canada.

D. They created national pride as the French became the envy of all Europe.

Plan your response. Make sure you understand the question. Here you must think about what Louis XIV accomplished—both good and bad.

6 What legacy did Louis XIV leave the French people?

Sample short response for question 6:

Louis XIV left the French people a mixed legacy. When he died, France was the most powerful country in Europe. Manufacturing had boomed and the economy had grown.

Louis had also expanded France's territory by fighting many wars. However, because he believed "L'état, c'est moi," he spent money extravagantly on himself while the French people lived in poverty and died on the battlefields. After his death, they would revolt.

Organize your ideas. Notice how the writer presents both sides of the king's legacy and supports statements with details and a quotation from the selection.

Reading Test Practice
LONG SELECTIONS

DIRECTIONS Now it's time to practice what you've learned about reading test items and choosing the best answers. Read the following selection, "They Don't Serve Fries with That." Use the side columns to make notes as you read the passage, focusing on: important ideas, comparisons and contrasts, causes and effects, difficult vocabulary, interesting details, questions you have, predictions you make, and conclusions you draw.

They Don't Serve Fries with That

When you think of French food, what comes to mind? If you're like most American teenagers, you probably said French fries. In fact, though, the *French* in the name refers not to the country where fries were invented, but to the way the potatoes are cut. Many people seem to agree that this worldwide favorite was first created in Belgium. So now you know what French food isn't. Let's take a look at what it is.

Beginnings of Haute Cuisine French food is no ordinary collection of calories. It is so special that it goes by the name *cuisine*, which in French means "kitchen," "cooking," and "cookery" as well as just "food." With the added adjectives *haute* ("high") or *grande* ("noble"), you get the idea that this food does more than just fill your stomach.

Haute cuisine originally was for the upper class and royalty. It differed from the food eaten by the peasants and bourgeois because it required expensive, high quality ingredients, a long time to prepare, and was served and eaten elegantly. It was brought to France in the early 16th century by the Italian noblewoman Catherine de Médicis. She introduced rare and expensive foods such as artichokes, truffles, and ice cream. The whole purpose of cooking became to bring out the natural flavor of foods and blend them to delight the eye as well as the taste buds.

Fancy dishes, glasses, and decorations were created to highlight the food, and table manners improved, too. One innovation—the fork—came into common use during the reign of Louis XIV, the extravagant Sun King.

Precision and Creativity Creating haute cuisine is a precise operation, and actually is as much a science as an art. Dishes are even named based on their ingredients or appearance. To us, for example, all edible hot liquids are just *soup*, but the French distinguish them as *consommé* (clear), *potage* (thick), or *crème* (cream).

Only the freshest ingredients go into haute cuisine. Fortunately, modern-day France has excellent farmland and good transportation so there's no problem getting meats, eggs, dairy products, vegetables, and fruits that are in perfect condition. Ingredients like wine and cheese that are best when aged are also available at their peak of perfection.

The methods of handling and preparing these high-quality ingredients are also specifically spelled out. What proportions of ingredients do you use? At what temperature do you cook them and for how long? How does roasting differ from braising and sautéing? Haute cuisine chefs have all the answers.

They also have plenty of room to express their creativity and artistry, though. Chefs try new combinations, add a pinch of this or a dash of that, and even tinker with the traditional cooking methods. Some experiments may fail, but others may improve the taste of a dish, cut the cooking time, or create totally new dishes.

Stocks and Sauces Traditional or not, all haute cuisine is based on cooking liquids called stocks. In fact, the French refer to them as *fonds de cuisine* or "the foundations of cooking." To make stocks, haute cuisine chefs spend hours browning bones, poultry, or fish in the oven. They then add carrots, onions, and herbs and simmer the mixture in water. As it simmers, they keep skimming off the fat, until it boils down to a fraction of its original volume. Only then is it ready to use for preparing or seasoning other foods.

One of the most important uses of stocks

is in making sauces. There are hundreds of French sauces, but, luckily, they can be grouped into broad categories. Three major categories are white, brown, and hollandaise. Each type of sauce has different ingredients and goes with different foods. Here are examples of each type and how they are prepared and served:

- White sauces—*béchamel, velouté, mornay, suprême*—Mix butter and flour; can add milk, cheese, herbs, or wine. Serve with poultry, fish, veal, or vegetables.
- Brown sauces—*ragoût, diable, piquant*—Simmer meat stock many hours and thicken with flour and milk cooked to turn brown; can add giblets, pickles, or spices. Serve with red meat, poultry, veal, or game.
- Hollandaise sauces—*béarnaise, mousseline*— Mix lemon juice and melted butter with warmed egg yolks; can add whipped cream, herbs, or wine. Serve with fish, eggs, or vegetables.

Nouvelle Cuisine and Beyond Traditional haute cuisine sticks to guidelines like these for making sauces. Since it is an art as well as a science, though, French cooking continues to change. One development is appropriately named *nouvelle* ("new") *cuisine*. It does away with thickened sauces and uses small portions of foods in unusual combinations.

Today, you can sample this new French cooking at restaurants across America and around the world. Tomorrow, who knows what heights haute cuisine will rise to? You can bet, though, that whatever form it takes, it won't include a side of fries.

Now answer questions 1–6. Base your answers on the selection "They Don't Serve Fries with That."

1 What is the author's main purpose in this selection?
- **A.** to persuade readers to eat French food
- **B.** to describe French haute cuisine
- **C.** to compare haute cuisine and *grande cuisine*
- **D.** to explain why people shouldn't eat French fries

2 Which of the following is NOT a goal of haute cuisine?
- **A.** enhancing foods' natural flavors
- **B.** pleasing peoples' eyes and stomachs
- **C.** smothering foods in sauces
- **D.** blending fresh ingredients that go together well

3 Where did haute cuisine begin?
- **A.** in Belgium
- **B.** in the Alps
- **C.** in France
- **D.** in Italy

4 How does *nouvelle cuisine* differ from haute cuisine?
- **A.** It is made from fresher ingredients.
- **B.** It uses smaller portions, more unusual combinations, and no thickened sauces.
- **C.** It involves not cooking foods as slowly to keep in their flavors.
- **D.** It is more expensive.

5 Why are stocks so important in haute cuisine?

A. They are used in making all sauces and in cooking other foods.

B. They take a long time to cook so people develop a good appetite.

C. They can be made from anything—bones, meat, poultry, fish, or vegetables.

D. They provide the money needed to pay for it.

6 What are some advantages and disadvantages of haute cuisine?

THINKING IT THROUGH

The notes in the side columns will help you think through your answers. See the answer key at the bottom of the next page. How well did you do?

Notice that answer choices C and D are based on misreadings of the selection. You can also eliminate the answer that may be the author's underlying purpose, but is not the main one.

1 What is the author's main purpose in this selection?

A. to persuade readers to eat French food

B. to describe French haute cuisine

C. to compare haute cuisine and *grande cuisine*

D. to explain why people shouldn't eat French fries

Read the question carefully, paying special attention to the word printed in capital letters.

2 Which of the following is NOT a goal of haute cuisine?

A. enhancing foods' natural flavors

B. pleasing peoples' eyes and stomachs

C. smothering foods in sauces

D. blending fresh ingredients that go together well

You can eliminate the answer choice that is not mentioned in the selection and the one that is not associated with haute cuisine. Skim the selection to decide between the other two choices.

3 Where did haute cuisine begin?

A. in Belgium

B. in the Alps

C. in France

D. in Italy

Notice that three of the answer choices include characteristics of haute cuisine that are not discussed about *nouvelle cuisine*.

4 How does *nouvelle cuisine* differ from haute cuisine?

A. It is made from fresher ingredients.

B. It uses smaller portions, more unusual combinations, and no thickened sauces

C. It involves not cooking foods as slowly to keep in their flavors.

D. It is more expensive.

5 Why are stocks so important in haute cuisine?

A. They are used in making all sauces and in cooking other foods.

B. They take a long time to cook so people develop a good appetite.

C. They can be made from anything—bones, meat, poultry, fish, or vegetables.

D. They provide the money needed to pay for it.

> Notice that answer choice C is true, but doesn't answer the question. Choice B can't be determined from the information given, and D is based on a different meaning of *stocks*.

6 What are some advantages and disadvantages of haute cuisine?

The main advantage of *haute cuisine* is that it uses fresh ingredients, which makes it healthy. It also is good to look at as well as to eat. Disadvantages are that you need to be a trained chef to make it right and that it takes a long time to cook. That means that it can't be made at home very easily. Because you have to get it at a restaurant, *haute cuisine* costs a lot. The fact that it's made from rare and high-quality foods makes it even more expensive.

> This is considered a strong response because it
> - directly addresses the question and stays on the topic.
> - supports statements with details from the selection.
> - draws logical conclusions.
> - is well-organized and clearly written.
> - uses correct grammar, punctuation, and spelling.

READING STRATEGIES FOR ASSESSMENT

Find the main idea and supporting details. Circle the main idea of the article. Then underline the details that support the main idea.

Use context clues. To discover what a "separatist" is, study the words and phrases around it. Which phrase helps define it?

Notice important details. Underline details that explain the importance of industry in Quebec.

Reading Test Model
SHORT SELECTIONS

DIRECTIONS "Canada's Many Cultures" is a short informative article. The strategies you have just learned can also help you with this shorter selection. As you read the selection, respond to the notes in the side column.

When you've finished reading, answer the multiple-choice questions. Use the side-column notes to help you understand what each question is asking and why each answer is correct.

Canada's Many Cultures

Canada's people come from different cultures, and many wish to safeguard their special language and customs. Some French-speaking Canadians are separatists, or people who want the province of Quebec to become an independent country. In 1980 and 1995, separatists asked for a vote on whether Quebec should become independent. Both times the issue was defeated, but the separatists promised to try again.

Quebec's Importance The federal government wants Quebec to remain part of Canada. Quebec is responsible for half of Canada's aerospace production, half of its information technology, and 38 percent of its high-tech industry. French culture is important in Canada's history and modern-day identity.

Laws Protecting Multiculturalism The Quebec provincial government has passed laws to preserve its citizens' French heritage. In an attempt to satisfy the separatists,

Canada's federal government passed the Canadian Multicultural Act in 1988. This act guarantees the right of all Canadians to preserve their cultural heritage. Finding ways to maintain a unified country remains a critical issue in Canada today.

1 Which of the following best describes the main idea of the article?

   A. Multiculturalism is important in Canada.

   B. The Canadian government wants Quebec to remain a part of Canada.

   C. People in Quebec speak French.

   D. Separatists do not want Quebec to remain a part of Canada.

Identify the focus. Each answer choice offers information from the article, but only one choice explains what the entire article is about.

2 What law did the Canadian federal government pass in 1988?

   A. The Canadian French Language Act

   B. The French Multicultural Act

   C. The French Heritage Act

   D. The Canadian Multicultural Act

Evaluate details. Think about what country the law affects, and what the subject of the article is. Which answer choice makes the most sense, given these two pieces of information?

3 What do separatists in Quebec want?

   A. Quebec to become an independent country

   B. Quebec to become a province of Canada

   C. Quebec to separate into pieces

   D. Quebec to be governed by separatists

Pay attention to the context of unfamiliar words. Find the sentence in the article where *separatist* is used. Notice that the information needed to make the correct choice can be found right next to the word *separatist* in the article.

Read the title. What does the title tell you the chart is about?

_____

_____

Read the labels. What do the labels on the left side of the chart tell you? What about the labels at the top of the chart?

_____

_____

ANSWER STRATEGIES

Read the question carefully. Notice that the question asks for the deepest lake, not necessarily the largest.

Read labels carefully. Make sure you understand which row presents information on Lake Huron.

Follow rows and columns carefully. If necessary, use your finger to trace across a row or down a column so that you don't accidentally wind up in the wrong place with the wrong information.

Answers:
1. A, 2. D, 3. A, 4. C, 5. D, 6. B

DIRECTIONS Some test questions ask you to analyze a visual rather than a reading selection. Study this chart carefully and answer the questions that follow.

The Great Lakes in Canada			
	Surface Area (sq. mi.)	Depth (feet/meters)	Elevation (feet/meters)
Lake Superior	11,100	1,330/405	600/183
Lake Huron	13,900	750/229	579/176
Lake Erie	4,930	210/64	570/174
Lake Ontario	3,880	802/244	245/75

4 What is the depth, in feet, of the deepest lake?
- **A.** 750
- **B.** 570
- **C.** 1,330
- **D.** 802

5 What is the surface area in Canada of Lake Huron?
- **A.** 4,930 square miles
- **B.** 11,100 square miles
- **C.** 1,330 square miles
- **D.** 13,900 square miles

6 At what altitude in meters is Lake Erie?
- **A.** 244 meters
- **B.** 174 meters
- **C.** 183 meters
- **D.** 579 meters

Reading Test Practice
SHORT SELECTIONS

DIRECTIONS Use the following selection to practice your skills. Read the paragraphs carefully. Then answer the multiple-choice questions that follow.

St. Martin: Two Islands in One

The island of St. Martin, one of the Antilles in the Caribbean Sea, is divided into two parts. One part (about two thirds of the island) is French, and one part (about one third) is Dutch. The Dutch call the island by the same name, but spell it differently: Sint Maarten. It is named for Saint Martin of Tours; Columbus sighted the island on the saint's feast day. The original treaty between the two countries was signed in 1648, but it was not until 1817 that the current boundaries were established.

Each side retains its own culture and language, but you don't need a passport to cross from one side to the other, and many people on both sides speak English. Caribbean culture is a strong influence on both sides of the island, and most island-born people speak Creole in addition to English, French, and Dutch. The French side of St. Martin is part of the *département* of Guadeloupe. Fishing and tourism are the main occupations there.

1. What was the author's purpose in writing this selection?

   A. to persuade the reader that St. Martin is a great place to visit

   B. to inform readers about the island of St. Martin

   C. to explain why St. Martin is divided into two parts

   D. to describe the history of the island of St. Martin

2. Which of the following is a conclusion you can draw from the selection?

   A. The French and Dutch have coexisted peacefully on the island since 1648.

   B. France discovered the island first.

   C. The boundaries on St. Martin have remained the same since 1817.

   D. The official language on both sides of the island is Dutch.

DIRECTIONS Use the graph below to answer the questions that follow.

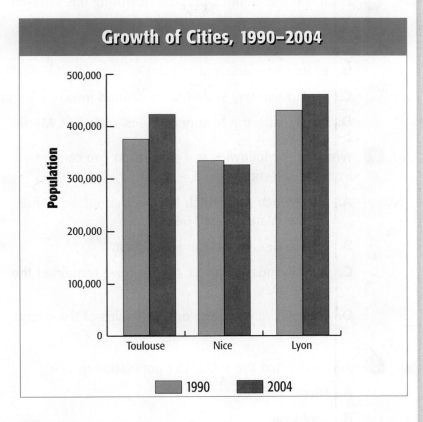

Growth of Cities, 1990–2004

■ 1990   ■ 2004

3 Which city had the SMALLEST population in 1990?

A. Nice

B. Toulouse

C. Lyon

4 Which city had the LARGEST population in 2004?

A. Nice

B. Toulouse

C. Lyon

5 Which city had the SMALLEST population increase between 1990 and 2004?

A. Nice

B. Toulouse

C. Lyon

THINKING IT THROUGH

1 What was the author's purpose in writing this selection?

First, read all of the answer choices. Then think carefully about the kind of information the article does and does not contain. The author's purpose will become clear.

   A. to persuade the reader that St. Martin is a great place to visit

   B. to inform readers about the island of St. Martin

   C. to explain why St. Martin is divided into two parts

   D. to describe the history of the island of St. Martin

2 Which of the following is a conclusion you can draw from the selection?

Ask yourself which of the answer choices is supported by information in the selection.

   A. The French and Dutch have coexisted peacefully on the island since 1648.

   B. France discovered the island first.

   C. The boundaries on St. Martin have remained the same since 1817.

   D. The official language on both sides of the island is Dutch.

3 Which city had the SMALLEST population in 1990?

Look at the key to determine which color denotes 1990. Then look for that color in the graph.

   A. Nice

   B. Toulouse

   C. Lyon

4 Which city had the LARGEST population in 2004?

The longest bar on the graph will give you the correct answer.

   A. Nice

   B. Toulouse

   C. Lyon

5 Which city had the SMALLEST population *increase* between 1990 and 2004?

The question asks you to compare 1990 with 2004. Look for the smallest positive difference in the two bars for each city to find the correct answer. Hint: Only two cities had population increases.

   A. Nice

   B. Toulouse

   C. Lyon

Answers:
1. B, 2. C, 3. A, 4. C, 5. C

Functional Reading Test Model

DIRECTIONS Study the following nutrition label from a package of chocolate-covered biscuits. Then answer the questions that follow.

Nutrition Facts

Serving Size 2 biscuits (25 g)
Servings Per Container 6

Amount Per Serving	
Calories 125	
Calories from Fat 55	

	% Daily Value*
Total Fat 6 g	10%
Saturated Fat 4 g	20%
Cholesterol 5 mg	2%
Sodium 50 mg	2%
Total Carbohydrate 15 g	
Dietary Fiber 2 g	8 %
Sugars 8 g	
Protein 2 g	

Vitamin A 0% • Vitamin C 0%
Calcium 0% • Iron 0%
* Percent Daily Values are based on a 2,000 calorie diet.

READING STRATEGIES FOR ASSESSMENT

Examine the structure of the label. Notice the types of information included in each of the four parts of the label.

Do the math. Remember that the "% Daily Value" and vitamin and mineral numbers on the label are for just a single serving.

ANSWER STRATEGIES

1 How many calories does this whole box of cookies contain?

To find the correct answer, multiply the number of calories per serving by the number of servings in the package.

   A. 825

   B. 750

   C. 700

   D. 800

2 If you ate two servings of cookies, how many milligrams of sodium would you consume?

Again, multiplication is the key to finding the correct answer.

   A. 50

   B. 75

   C. 100

   D. 200

3 Are chocolate-covered biscuits a smart food choice for people trying to limit their fat intake?

To answer this question, just look at the part of the label that tells how much fat each serving contains.

   A. No, because each serving has 6 grams of fat.

   B. Yes, because the serving size is just two cookies.

   C. No, because they have 125 calories per serving.

   D. Yes, because they have 50 milligrams of sodium per serving.

Answers:
1. B, 2. C, 3. A

DIRECTIONS Study the following travel advertisement for a vacation package to Tahiti. Circle the information that you think is most important. Then answer the multiple-choice questions that follow.

EXPERIENCE THE EXCITEMENT OF

TAHITI!

Snorkeling! Windsurfing! Sailing! Golf!
First-Class Entertainment!

4 days/3 nights at the
Tahiti Adventure Resort

only **$689** per person
airfare included *

Adventure Resort Package also includes
continental breakfast, two beach passes,
two spa treatments

*Price based on double occupancy. Airfare from
New York City only. From Chicago add $175. From
Los Angeles add $350. Single travelers add $200.

1 Which of the following is NOT included in the $689 price?

   A. beach passes

   B. windsurfing

   C. spa treatments

   D. continental breakfast

2 How much will this vacation package cost a single traveler from Los Angeles?

   A. $479

   B. $1,029

   C. $1,239

   D. $689

3 For which of the following is this vacation package the LEAST expensive per person?

   A. two sisters from New York

   B. a stockbroker from Los Angeles

   C. a single traveler from New York

   D. a college student from Chicago

THINKING IT THROUGH

The notes in the side column will help you think through your answers. Check the answer key at the bottom of this page. How well did you do?

> Although the ad mentions windsurfing prominently, it does not indicate that this activity is included in the price.

1 Which of the following is NOT included in the $689 price?

A. beach passes

B. windsurfing

C. spa treatments

D. continental breakfast

> To answer this question, read the small type at the bottom of the ad and add the extra charges to the advertised price. Double occupancy means two people staying in the same room.

2 How much will this vacation package cost a single traveler from Los Angeles?

A. $479

B. $1,029

C. $1,239

D. $689

> Read each answer choice carefully. How many people are traveling? Where are they coming from? Then use the information in the ad to determine who will get the best deal.

3 For which of the following is this vacation package the LEAST expensive per person?

A. two sisters from New York

B. a stockbroker from Los Angeles

C. a single traveler from New York

D. a college student from Chicago

Answers:
1.B, 2.C, 3.A

Revising-and-Editing Test Model

DIRECTIONS Read the following paragraph carefully. Then answer the multiple-choice questions that follow. After answering the questions, read the material in the side columns to check your answer strategies.

READING STRATEGIES FOR ASSESSMENT

Watch for common errors. Highlight or underline errors such as incorrect spelling or punctuation, fragments or run-on sentences, and missing or misplaced information.

¹Paris, the capital of France. ²It is home to one of that nations cultural treasures—the Louvre museum. ³The building was constructed in the thirteenth century as a fortress. ⁴Then they opened it there in 1783 today it has over 500,000 square feet of exhibition space. ⁵The museum is located on a street called the Rue de Rivoli. ⁶Their are many famous works of art they're, including the Venus de Milo and the Mona Lisa.

ANSWER STRATEGIES

1. Which sentence in the paragraph is actually a fragment, an incomplete thought?

   A. sentence 1

   B. sentence 3

   C. sentence 4

   D. sentence 5

Incomplete Sentences A sentence is a group of words that has a subject and a verb and expresses a complete thought. If either the subject or the verb is missing, the group of words is an incomplete sentence.

2. In sentence 2, which of the following is the correct possessive form of the word *nation*?

   A. nation's

   B. nations's

   C. nations'

   D. nations

Possessive Nouns In sentence 2, the word *nation* is singular. So, it takes the singular possessive form.

3 What is the best way to rewrite the first part of sentence 4?

   A. Then he decided to change it to an art museum

   B. In 1783, the government opened the first state museum there

   C. Then in 1783, they made it into the first state museum

   D. After a while, they decided to open a big art museum there

4 Which sentence in the paragraph is a run-on sentence?

   A. sentence 1

   B. sentence 2

   C. sentence 4

   D. sentence 5

5 What is the best way to rewrite the first part of sentence 6?

   A. They're many famous works of art their

   B. They're are many famous works of art their

   C. There are many famous works of art there

   D. Their are many famous works of art there

6 Sentence 5 is out of place. Where should sentence 5 occur?

   A. after sentence 2

   B. before sentence 2

   C. after sentence 6

   D. after sentence 3

Answers:
1.A, 2.A, 3.B, 4.C, 5.C, 6.A

Revising-and-Editing Test Practice

DIRECTIONS Read the following paragraph carefully. As you read, circle each error that you find and identify the error in the side column—for example, misspelled word or incorrect punctuation. When you have finished, circle the letter of the correct choice for each question that follows.

¹On May, 22, 1885, one of the most greatest writers in French history died. ²He was born in Besançon. ³As a young man, Victor Hugo writes poetry and helped found a literary magazine. ⁴In 1831 his novel. ⁵*Notre Dame de Paris*, known in English as *The Hunchback of Notre Dame*, was published. ⁶He also wrote many successful plays and other works, he was elected to the *Academie Française* in 1841.

1 Which sentence in the paragraph is a fragment?
A. sentence 2
B. sentence 4
C. sentence 5
D. sentence 6

2 What is the correct way to write the date in sentence 1?
A. May/22/1885
B. May 22 1885
C. May 22, 1885
D. May, 22 1885

3 In sentence 1, which of the following is the correct form of the superlative adjective?

A. greatest

B. greater

C. more great

D. more greatest

4 Which of the following errors occurs in sentence 2?

A. unclear pronoun reference

B. incorrect capitalization

C. incorrect punctuation

D. incorrect verb tense

5 Which of the following is the correct way to rewrite the first part of sentence 3?

A. As a young man, Victor Hugo wrote poetry and helps found

B. As a young man, Victor Hugo is writing poetry and helped found

C. As a young man, Victor Hugo wrote poetry and is helping found

D. As a young man, Victor Hugo wrote poetry and helped found

6 Which of the following is the best way to punctuate the middle of sentence 6?

A. plays and other works, he was elected

B. plays and other works. He was elected

C. plays and other works—and he was elected

D. plays, and other works, and, he was elected

THINKING IT THROUGH

Use the notes in the side columns to help you understand why some answers are correct and others are not. Check the answer key on the next page. How well did you do?

1 Which sentence in the paragraph is a fragment?

A. sentence 2

B. sentence 4

C. sentence 5

D. sentence 6

> Remember that a sentence has a subject and a verb and expresses a complete thought. Which sentence is lacking either a subject or a verb?

2 What is the correct way to write the date in sentence 1?

A. May/22/1885

B. May 22 1885

C. May 22, 1885

D. May, 22 1885

> When writing a date, the name of the month should be spelled out, and the day and year should be separated by a comma.

3 In sentence 1, which of the following is the correct form of the superlative adjective?

A. greatest

B. greater

C. more great

D. more greatest

> A superlative adjective is formed by adding –*est* to the adjective or placing the word *most* before the adjective. Never do both at the same time.

First check to be sure that words are capitalized correctly, that the sentence is punctuated correctly, and that the verb has the same tense as other verbs in the paragraph. Then ask, "Who is *he*?" Unless you can answer that question with a proper name, the pronoun reference is unclear.

Remember that all the verbs in a paragraph should agree—that is, have the same tense. So both verbs in sentence 3 must agree.

Remember that a run-on sentence is two or more complete thoughts joined without correct punctuation. One solution is to create separate sentences.

4 Which of the following errors occurs in sentence 2?

A. unclear pronoun reference

B. incorrect capitalization

C. incorrect punctuation

D. incorrect verb tense

5 Which of the following is the correct way to rewrite the first part of sentence 3?

A. As a young man, Victor Hugo wrote poetry and helps found

B. As a young man, Victor Hugo is writing poetry and helped found

C. As a young man, Victor Hugo wrote poetry and is helping found

D. As a young man, Victor Hugo wrote poetry and helped found

6 Which of the following is the best way to punctuate the middle of sentence 6?

A. plays and other works; and he was elected

B. plays and other works. He was elected

C. plays and other works—and he was elected

D. plays, and other works, and, he was elected

Writing Test Model

DIRECTIONS Many tests ask you to write an essay in response to a writing prompt. A writing prompt is a brief statement that describes a writing situation. Some writing prompts ask you to explain *what, why,* or *how.* Others ask you to convince someone of something.

As you analyze the following writing prompts, read and respond to the notes in the side columns. Then look at the response to each prompt. The notes in the side columns will help you understand why each response is considered strong.

Prompt A

Some child-rearing experts believe that young people should be kept busy after school and on the weekends with a variety of structured activities, such as music lessons, sports, dance classes, and so on. Others say that young people today have been "overscheduled" and need more time to themselves—to read, think about the future, and even just to daydream.

Think about your experiences and the way your non-school time is structured. Do you think lots of structure, more personal time, or a combination of the two is most beneficial to young people? Remember to provide solid reasons and examples for the position you take.

Strong Response

Today was a typical day for my little brother Jeff. He got up at five o'clock to go to the local ice rink for hockey practice. Then he was off to school. At the end of the school day,

ANALYZING THE PROMPT

Identify the focus. What issue will you be writing about? Circle the focus of your essay in the first sentence of the prompt.

Understand what's expected of you. First, circle what the prompt asks you to do. Then identify your audience. What kinds of details will appeal to this audience?

ANSWER STRATEGIES

Capture the reader's interest. The writer begins by describing a typical busy day in his younger brother's life.

Jeff had a piano lesson followed by a meeting of his Cub Scout troop. After a quick dinner, he did homework for two hours. He finally got to bed at ten o'clock. That's a lot to pack into a single day, especially since Jeff is just seven years old! I think that in addition to sports, music, and other activities, kids like Jeff need some time to themselves.

Many parents, mine included, think a busy kid is a safe kid. They believe that the less time a kid has on his hands, the less likely he'll wind up doing something he shouldn't be doing or being with people he shouldn't be with. That's probably true for many kids. After all, it's hard to get into trouble when you spend every day being carpooled from one activity to another.

But some busy kids do get into trouble anyway. Jeff's friend Mark got caught trying to shoplift a CD last weekend, and he's involved in just as many activities as Jeff is. So having a busy schedule is no guarantee that a kid won't get into trouble.

Plus, I think kids benefit from having free time to go to the movies, play video games, read, or even just be by themselves. Growing up isn't always easy, and kids need some time alone to figure things out, think about what's important to them, and decide what they really want to do.

Last Saturday afternoon, Jeff's soccer practice was canceled because of thunderstorms. We went to see a movie and later spent some time talking and listening to music in my room. It was the first time in months that we had time just to hang out together, and we really enjoyed it. Jeff said it was like having a day off. I think more kids like Jeff could use a day off too.

State the position clearly. The last sentence of the first paragraph makes the writer's position clear to the reader. Now the writer can spend the rest of the essay developing his argument.

Address opposing views. The writer brings up an opposing view—that busy kids are less likely to get into trouble—and admits that it might sometimes be true.

Use good examples to support the position. Here, the writer uses an example to make the point that not all busy kids stay out of trouble.

Use logical reasoning to further develop the position. The writer offers logical reasons why free time is important.

Restate the position in the conclusion. Using another concrete example, the writer restates his position that kids need some time to themselves.

Prompt B

Depending on where you live, each season of the year can be very different than it is in other parts of the country. Which season do you enjoy the most—summer, autumn, winter, or spring? What is that season like in your part of the country? What makes it special to you?

ANALYZING THE PROMPT

Look for the main idea. The first few sentences of the prompt present the subject you will write about. Try restating the subject in your own words.

Understand what's expected of you. What does the prompt ask you to do? Explain something? Persuade someone? State your personal feelings?

Strong Response

Here in the upper Midwest, the seasons seem as different from one another as night and day. Summer usually arrives suddenly. The temperatures soar, the humidity rises, and fierce thunderstorms add drama and sometimes destruction to the season. Autumn brings a crisp, cool, and colorful change as the leaves turn golden and the air turns chilly. Winter can be bitterly cold, and heavy snows often make the simple trip to school a real ordeal.

Then comes spring. Spring is a truly magical time of the year. I can sense spring long before it actually arrives. There's a certain scent in the air, and something is different about the way the sunlight looks. Soon the winter snows are reduced to muddy puddles. The tree branches swell with buds, and the first green shoots of crocus and tulip leaves struggle up out of the ground. Most magical of all, the early morning hours just after dawn are filled with the cries of migrating birds heading back north.

Because my family lives in a small community surrounded by farmland, I get to experience a different kind of spring than many people do. The fields behind our house fill up with wildflowers that season the air with perfume and color. A trip to Jefferson's Pond offers a chance to watch ducks and geese resting on their long

ANSWER STRATEGIES

Create an intriguing introduction. The writer arouses the reader's curiosity by leaving out one of the four seasons.

Include specific details. The writer uses specific details about each season to make the description vivid.

Include the kind of information the prompt asks for. Notice how the writer follows the directions in the prompt by explaining what spring is like in her part of the country.

Use sensory details. Details that appeal to the reader's sense of sight, sound, and smell bring the description to life.

seasonal journeys. The apple and cherry trees at the McKlintock family orchards explode with blossoms until they look like giant balls of cotton candy.

Mostly, however, I love spring because it is a season of hope. The earth is coming back to life, filled with possibilities. I feel like I am, too.

Writing Test Practice

DIRECTIONS Read the following writing prompt. Using the strategies you've learned in this section, analyze the prompt, plan your response, and then write an essay explaining your position.

Prompt C

You have volunteered to participate in your community's semiannual blood drive. Your task is to write a letter to your community newspaper encouraging everyone in town to consider giving blood.

Think about all the ways your community benefits from having an adequate blood supply. Write a letter that explains what these benefits are. Include specific examples. End your letter by appealing to your fellow citizens' sense of civic pride and duty.

Scoring Rubrics

DIRECTIONS Use the following checklist to see whether you have written a strong persuasive essay. You will have succeeded if you can check nearly all of the items.

The Prompt

☐ My response meets all the requirements stated in the prompt.

☐ I have stated my position clearly and supported it with details.

☐ I have addressed the audience appropriately.

☐ My essay fits the type of writing suggested in the prompt (letter to the editor, article for the school paper, and so on).

Reasons

☐ The reasons I offer really support my position.

☐ My audience will find the reasons convincing.

☐ I have stated my reasons clearly.

☐ I have given at least three reasons.

☐ I have supported my reasons with sufficient facts, examples, quotations, and other details.

☐ I have presented and responded to opposing arguments.

☐ My reasoning is sound. I have avoided faulty logic.

Order and Arrangement

☐ I have included a strong introduction.

☐ I have included a strong conclusion.

☐ The reasons are arranged in a logical order.

Word Choice

☐ The language of my essay is appropriate for my audience.

☐ I have used precise, vivid words and persuasive language.

Fluency

☐ I have used sentences of varying lengths and structures.

☐ I have connected ideas with transitions and other devices.

☐ I have used correct spelling, punctuation, and grammar.

Credits

Acknowledgments

"Sur le fil à sécher le linge" by Corrine Albaut. Text copyright © by Corrine Albaut. Reprinted by permission of Corrine Albaut.

Photography

23 (br) ©Andia/Alamy Images; **93** (b) ©Corbis; **97** (tl) © Corbis; **97** (tr) ©Emmanuel Lattes/Alamy; **103** (tr) ©Redmond Durrell/Alamy Images; **107** (tl) Photodisc/Getty Images; **109** (br) ©North Wind Picture Archives/Alamy Images; **113** (cl) ©Urbanhearts/Fotolia.

All other photos by Lawrence Migdale/PIX/McDougal Littell/ Houghton Mifflin Co.